I0141638

VERY GRATEFUL

The Story of My
Hundred-Year-Old
Mother and Me

Janet Ross Eberman, 1918

Very Grateful

The Story of My
Hundred-Year-Old
Mother and Me

Bobbi Fisher

VG PRESS
Sudbury, Massachusetts

Copyright © 2015 by Bobbi Fisher
All rights reserved
Designed by Helen Robinson

First edition

This work is licensed only for use by the original
purchaser. Making copies of this work or
distributing it to any unauthorized person by any
means, including without limit email, file transfer,
paper printout, or any other method, is a violation
of international copyright law.

ISBN 978-0-692-48821-8 (paperback: alk. paper)
ISBN 978-0-692-49906-1 (ebook)

VG PRESS
Sudbury, Massachusetts

To my sisters, Alice and Margot, and my brother, Ross

Janet Ross Eberman, 2011

On September 17, 2011, thirteen days before my mother died, at the age of one hundred and one, I wrote on a piece of paper for her the following words: "God has been with you all of your life."

Mom was in her wheelchair, and my husband, Jim, and I were sitting on a bench in the little garden of the facility where she had been living for the past nine months.

Mom, whose hearing had been poor for years but who could still read without her glasses, looked deliberately at what I had written. Although she was slowing down mentally, with effort the synapses in her brain still connected.

"It's true," she said as she nodded her head and pursed her lips.

But she wasn't finished. After another pause, she offered her final words, "Very grateful."

She never spoke again, but she didn't need to; those two words summed up her life.

Preface

This book celebrates my mother's life of grace and gratitude and tells the story of our last two years together—Mom, in her twilight years, and I, turning seventy.

During her last two years, as she had always done, Mom showed not only to me but to everyone who knew her that it is through gratitude that we lead a meaningful life and come to a peaceful end. Her Christian faith gave her a way of coping and struggling, of experiencing pleasure and delight, of accepting joys and hardships, and of choosing only to love, which she did by reaching out to others.

I have vivid images of Mom, lips closed, head cocked and nodding, eye to eye, listening to someone while standing on the church steps after a service, at family gatherings in Brooklyn, at home when people were visiting, with the clerk at the grocery store or a friend on the street or the person cleaning our hotel room when we traveled. It was her demeanor, not her words, that showed her compassion. Mom didn't see these encounters in big ways, but the recipients never forgot them.

She told me once, "I am more interested in doing things, not thinking about them so much or why I'm doing them. I'm a people person. Having been through loss, I think I know that people can't just sit home and feel sorry for themselves, because there are too many other people who've had even greater losses. You have to help where you can, and your experience makes a difference—or should."

She intuited what someone needed at a particular moment, she was drawn to other people's interests, she had an innate ability to make them feel knowledgeable and important, and she could always smile. Her volunteer jobs, at Norfolk Hospital and at Waveny Care Center, a nursing and rehabilitation facility, were important to her and, she said, good for her.

"Sometimes, sure, it would be easier not to go and stay home instead, but I get more out of it than I ever put into it. It is rewarding. I thank God I can walk in and walk out. Who knows, some year I might be there and I would like to see somebody from the outside, too. You can't just selfishly think or pretend there aren't any people who are sick or dying; it's what's going on, it's what's happening. And why are we here? That's one reason. I think we're here to reach out to other people. It's part of my Christian faith. It all fits together."

How prophetic. Fifteen years later Mom moved to Waveny Care Center, where she spent the last nine months of her life, welcoming visitors, reaching out with her smile.

As I accompanied Mom toward her death, she also accompanied me toward a future without her. There was a life-sustaining affinity between us. She was the most important person in my life. We had always provided confidence, purpose, and companionship to each other, but as she was fading away, I realized that soon I would be on my own in my longing for God and my search for faith. As Mom was failing physically and mentally, I was struggling with ways to balance my love of family and friends with my growing desire for solitude. The child in me didn't want Mom to leave; the new grown-up in me wondered what my life would be like without my mother and our uncomplicated, undemanding, effortless, and yet powerful relationship.

During Mom's last two years of life, I kept a journal. I wrote at home in my little study (which my grandchildren have affectionately named the angel room) and I wrote at the cottage by the sea that I rented in the winter. I wrote about Mom, I wrote about me, and I wrote about the two of us together. The daily entries I made are the basis of *Very Grateful*, along with a brief biography of Mom's first ninety-nine years, quotations from two recorded interviews I conducted with Mom in 1995, and some current (2015) reflections about what I learned from her and what it is like for me now. I've also included some of the "Mom reports" I wrote to my siblings after each visit, and the emailed notes I sent to Mom at both the New Canaan Inn retirement residence and the Waveny Care Center.

Living to age one hundred and one is not my goal, but for Mom and for those who knew her, certainly for me, it was perfect. She was in good health, never a burden, always grateful. When there were no more words, her smile expressed gratitude; at the end her gaze was one of expectation and awe, and then she let go and moved on.

Janet Ross Eberman

There is a time for everything, and a season
for every activity under the heavens.
—Ecclesiastes 3:1

My mother was born Janet Appleton Ross on May 8, 1910, in Brooklyn, New York, the third and last child of loving parents Winifred Appleton Ross and Donald Ross. She had a happy childhood growing up in Brooklyn with her older sister and brother, Kath and Don. She attended Packer Collegiate Institute, within walking distance of her home, and then went on to Vassar College, where she majored in English. Mom had it all; she was smart, popular, and pretty, but most important she was endowed with a hopeful, positive disposition, so apparent in photographs taken of her throughout her life.

Mom described her beginnings in a recorded interview:

> I was born on Vanderbilt Avenue, in Brooklyn,
> and the family moved when I was about two to
> 100 Gates Avenue, where I lived until we moved
> to 1 Pierrepont Street when I was out of college.
> I only lived in three places before I was married.
> I was born at home, in a brownstone house.
> Fifty dollars they paid Dr. Fisk. That was all,
> for the care of my mother, the delivery, and the
> postpartum. Fifty dollars and he of course came
> to the house and delivered me. Don't remember
> that [*chuckle*].

At the end of her senior year at Vassar her beloved father committed suicide, allegedly a victim of the Great Depression. According to Mom he had been a fun, loving, always present father. To the end of her life Mom couldn't believe he had "left them that way":

> I think of the time after my father died when I came down from Vassar. I was in my senior year and went to the Met with Mimi. I don't know what the opera was; it might have been *Lohengrin*. But I remember that was one way we saw each other, and of course I was very concerned about her; but also, being twenty and a senior in college and interested in getting through that year, I maybe didn't pay as much attention to the sorrow she must have been going through.
>
> However, I think one reason she handled that tragedy so well was that she was needed by her parents, Gram and Gramps. She then was making plans to sell 100 Gates Avenue and come and live with them at the lovely apartment in Brooklyn and be, as it were, a housekeeper for them.
>
> I never felt that she felt it was her fault or that she should have known ahead. I do remember, however, that after my father's death the minister of my church came to call on her before the service, and she did say to me and maybe to Kath and Don that he was not very helpful, that he didn't help her understand why this had happened or why she didn't see my father's depression, didn't know that this was a possibility. . . .
>
> I think that a lot of people were overextended financially and worried about it. I

think that the fact that my father did of course
have to examine this building, it provided
him an opportunity. Maybe he had planned
ahead of time to take his life by falling off the
building. During this time and from '29 there
was the Depression. The Depression, capital D!
People were taking their lives because they were
overextended; they couldn't take it. Business was
very poor and they were in trouble and some
people couldn't handle it.

So it was not unusual, but from the letters
that I got at the time, and from my friends who
came to see me and give me their sympathy,
everyone had lovely things to say about my father.
They loved him. He was the kind of friend's father
that you liked to have; he was very kind. That
was the adjective describing him, kind in almost
every letter.

We all have difficulties, but we have to
leave them behind and do the best we can and be
thankful.

She did just that. Putting her father's death behind her, after
college Mom returned to Brooklyn and got a job in New York
City, where she met my dad. Here is how she recalled it:

Oh, we met in business. I was working as a
secretary and he came on as art director of *Arts
and Decoration* magazine. We were all women in
the office. One day I went up to 578 Madison
Avenue, where *Arts and Decoration* was being
assembled and, as they say, being put to bed—
that means it's going to press. I came in and
said, "Is there anything I can do to help?" and

that's the first thing Papa remembers me saying, and he said that turned out to be very typical of me [*chuckle*]. So he called me for a date and I couldn't accept the invitation he wanted and then he pursued it and then we did have dinner. We began to see each other a lot.

According to Dad, "In walked this beautiful young woman who said, 'Hi, how can I help?' I told myself that that was the girl for me." And she was. A year and a half later, on October 12, 1935, Janet Appleton Ross married Edwin Eberman, Jr., five years her senior.

My older sister, Alice Hopkins Eberman, was born on September 5, 1937. I, Barbara Perry Eberman, followed on December 30, 1939. Two years later we moved from Brooklyn and settled in a rental house in New Canaan, Connecticut. Dad commuted to New York City. I have vivid wartime memories of school buses taking commuters to the train station, as well as buses on Sunday transporting families to and from church. There we were, out in the country, five miles from town, Mom, Dad, Alice, and me, along with Amber, our liver-spotted Dalmatian.

It was a compact little family; the four of us ice skating on Mud Pond, raking the yard in the fall, eating at the kitchen table, wrapping Christmas presents, and occasionally driving to Brooklyn to visit my grandmother Mimi and the aunts, uncles, and cousins we had left behind. Life was good to Alice and me and to our parents.

Many of my memories of that time are of playing alone in the yard and woods around the house, happy in my own world. In one particular memory I am jumping in the leaves, oblivious that I was supposed to be helping Dad with the raking. Mom was inside preparing a meal or very likely baking cookies for someone but also saving some for the snack she would have ready for us when we came in. I picture her graceful and easy, never complaining, always smiling, but also purposeful and serious. As a young mother, as well as during the years before and after, she was a rare spirit, always radiating love.

I have another memory from these early childhood days, of an incident between Mom and me that I believe bonded us forever. We were at home together; my older sister, Alice, was in school. It was naptime, Mom napping in her room, I taking my quiet hour in the guestroom. Not wanting to disturb her, I tiptoed into the hall and then into the bathroom that separated the two bedrooms, pulled up the little bathroom stepstool, and started rummaging in the medicine closet—not for very long, no more than thirty seconds. Then I went back into the hall and sat outside her door, waiting. After what seemed an eternity, Mom emerged from her room to find me sitting there. Then this:

Mom, in a steady, matter-of-fact but sad voice: "I heard you in the medicine closet."

I looked right at her but no words came.

Mom: "You know you're not supposed to go in there. Don't ever do it again.

Me, in a very soft voice: "I'm sorry; I won't; I promise."

That was the end of the conversation. Mom never brought it up again, nor did I. But it remains my first and most important childhood memory, always coupled with an image of me contentedly playing alone outside in the yard. Perhaps this composite memory sums up the independence of my childhood, Mom somewhere in the background, keeping an eye on me for safety but leaving me alone, never intruding but always an available presence, I doing the same for her.

I learned later that Mom was resting from a miscarriage, having lost a baby at full term, a boy with Down syndrome. I was looking for something to make her better, which I found not in the medicine closet but in our being together. On that very day, as I looked at her through my three-year-old eyes, I may have silently promised to make her happy forever.

The sadness of a miscarriage didn't, however, disturb our life. As the years went by Mom's only reference to it was her story that Alice, age five, had asked, "Doesn't God want us to be happy?" to which Mom had replied, "I was so grateful that I had two healthy children to come home to."

That was Mom's way. When I commented to her that our family doesn't always pour everything out, that we take the good and the bad and move on, she said, "Yes, that's the way it is. It's better; it's better not to keep examining or analyzing everything to death. Sometimes I think it's a good way to do it, to move on. Don't you?"

Life went on as usual for the four of us until Mom was pregnant again and my parents bought a house across town. I have no recollection of the time or events leading up to the move, but I vividly remember her sitting on the edge of my bed giving me her full attention on that first night in our new home. I was five and a half, in my own bedroom with pink-and-white wallpaper, patterned triangles filled with idyllic country family scenes. No more sharing a room with my sister.

During one of the interviews Mom mentioned that she valued having one's own room:

> At Gates Avenue I had a room of my own and
> I loved that. I think children like to feel they
> have their own room, don't you? It's not always
> possible, but you can do what you want in your
> own room. When you were growing up, see how
> much nicer it was for you and Alice not to be in
> the same room? You had to share the bathroom,
> and when you traveled, of course, you had to be
> together.

With the move to a bigger house, our compact little family was a thing of the past. Margot Ross Eberman was born on December 30, 1945, on my sixth birthday; my brother, Ross Eberman, followed a year and a half later, on August 17, 1947. Mom had a household to run, a husband to attend to, and with six years between Margot and me, two sets of kids to manage: when I was in sixth grade, Margot was just in kindergarten; when Alice was a senior, Ross was a second grader.

The spring before Ross was born, Molly Singleton arrived from Winter Park, Florida, to help. Her plan was to stay for six months to earn enough money to pay for dentures and then return to Florida in the fall. She did that but came back to us for twenty-five summers. At the end of every October, we would *beg* her to stay through the winter, but she never did, she always had to get home to vote.

Along with my parents, each of us kids had a special relationship with Molly. At the end of the day one of us would be in her room chatting away. I have memories of Mom and Molly sitting at the kitchen table discussing the menu for the week. I've always considered Molly, who called Mom "sweetie," one of Mom's best friends.

During the years I was growing up we attended the Congregational Church of New Canaan. Every Sunday we went to church, Sunday school, youth group, whatever was on the calendar. On Christmas morning we left our presents and their wrappings on the floor to attend the Christmas Day service. Among the twenty or so people who showed up at the little chapel, we were the only kids. We wanted to stay home, but for Mom and Dad attending church, especially on Christmas, was an important expression of their faith. Dad once told me that there was no way to prove the "truth" of Christianity, but following Jesus was the best way he knew to help him lead a good life.

My parents shared their faith through the Christmas

card they sent each year. I have copies of all the ones Dad created, from the first, in 1947, to the final one, in 1986. They are works of art, Dad's drawings in his favorite medium, pen and ink. The first was a single drawing with a simple message. Over the years he began to add pages, develop a theme (bridges, doors, gardens), and write an accompanying message. Although the drawing, calligraphy, and message were Dad's creations, the card was a joint venture because Mom was the keeper of the list, and a big list it was. One year they sent three hundred and fifty cards.

I have every index card Mom filled out, over seven hundred, one for each person or family to whom Mom and Dad sent a card and then for the recipients during the twenty years after Dad died. A history of sixty years of friendships.

Mom wrote or typed the person's name, last name first for easy filing (for couples it would be Mr. and Mrs.), then the address. At the bottom she wrote the last two digits of the year, then circled this number when a card was received in return. And people responded; they loved my parents and they wanted one of those Ed Eberman cards. Over the years Mom added other pertinent information: births, deaths, marriages, divorces, and toward the end, visits people made to her at the Inn. If someone moved, she crossed out the address and added the current one. When the front and back were filled, she stapled a new card to the original. When her wooden file box got too full, she got another box and re-sorted the cards, moving the cards of those who had died or for whom contact was lost to the archive box. She kept those boxes in her desk, ready to read and review.

Addressing the cards took place in the living room, beginning right after Thanksgiving. "We are through the Js," Mom would announce. Then, about a week before Christmas, when they were "through the Zs," Dad would take boxes and boxes of cards to the post office. Those going "overseas" were sent early.

The Christmas card ritual continued as we grew up, graduated from college, married, had children, and followed careers.

Dad retired at age sixty to paint, garden, and contribute designs for the memorial garden at church and the gardens at both the New Canaan Inn and Waveny Care Center. Mom volunteered at church, Norwalk Hospital, and Waveny. My parents traveled all over the world.

Our growing families gathered at Grammy and Papa's for holidays and family get-togethers. Mom and Dad held court around the dining room table, welcoming each member of the next generation as he or she sat in the family highchair before graduating to a booster seat at the big round table. Leaves were added to make room for new additions to the family. Grammy, as she was called, always sat right next to Papa, her husband. It was at that table that relationships between grandchildren and grandparents were formed and nurtured. The years went by, and Grammy and Papa were soon receiving tickets for their grandchildren's high school graduations.

When Dad told us that he had prostate cancer, I knew that my life would change, that the stability of my forty-five years would shift. Two and a half years later, with Mom as his generous caregiver, Dad passed away.

The last time I saw him, six weeks before his death, he showed me the final Christmas card. He had planned it knowing it would be sent posthumously. After he died, I visited Mom that December to help her address, stuff, seal, stamp, and take the cards to the post office. I don't think it was easy for her, but it brought forth her mettle. She wanted to follow his wishes. And she did, with her own insert, in her own words:

As you may know, Ed died at the age of eighty-one on August 15, 1986, after putting up a gallant fight against cancer. He had a wonderful life. One of the last projects he completed was this year's Christmas card, and I feel that he wanted me to have it printed and sent to you, our friends.

The card was composed of twelve drawings and messages written by Dad, one for each month. The drawings were all of things around our home, except for December, which was of the church, and included Dad's final blessing:

Thus, day by day, we've come full cycle through years of Decembers singing carols on the green to celebrate that day we joyously call Christmas. To you we again say carpe diem—seize the day—for each one can be wonderfully kind and miraculous.

Mom was grateful his suffering was over. As she told us, "I did a lot of grieving while Dad was still alive. And besides, I'm grateful for the fifty years we had together." And in her usual way, she moved on.

The following Christmas, Mom bought UNICEF cards and began her own tradition, which included a prayer or poem or one of her own messages. The cards were commercial, the message, hers. She worked from the list she and Dad had started, but it was always changing as people died, contact was lost, and new names were added. Through the years Mom continued to live in the present, to seize the day.

Before we knew it, Grammy was cheering as her grandchildren received their college diplomas. She loved to tell us how grateful she was to get to know them as adults, all eleven of them: Alice's five, Janet, Gail, Dwight, Amy, and Linda; my two, Tim and Emily; Margot's two, Sarah and Matt; and Ross's two, Jody and Kristin. Although Dad died two years after Jody was born, he stood as godfather at her baptism at the same church where we gathered to remember him, just two months before Kristin, his final grandchild, was born. Through the ensuing years, Mom was able to spend some time with her two youngest granddaughters, and lived long enough to know they had graduated from college.

Five years after Dad died, Mom sold the Wahackme Road house and bought a condo in town, where she lived for ten years. She continued volunteering, entertained friends for tea and supper, and gave herself a ninetieth birthday party. I visited her at least once a month from my home in Massachusetts. We would sit and talk over a glass of Cinzano, she would serve me a meal, and then we would do the dishes.

During that period, Mom and I traveled to Scotland and Italy together. Her last trip abroad was to her granddaughter Sarah's wedding, in France, in 2001. It was then that I realized I didn't want the responsibility of caring for her in a foreign country, but I also sensed that she was ready to stay close to home. She had sold her condo by then and was living at the New Canaan Inn. "I have so many memories," she would tell me.

Those first five years at the Inn were especially happy ones for Mom. She drove until she was ninety-five, went to church every Sunday, participated in Bible study, continued with as many volunteer commitments as she could manage, and attended her weekly sewing group meetings and the monthly intergenerational book group composed of women and men, singles and couples. She did her best to stay active and to keep up with friends. She sent birthday and Christmas cards until she was ninety-eight.

I remember vividly the December day in 2008 when Mom said no to sending cards. (Alice, Margot, and I had tried to dissuade her the year before, but she wasn't ready to stop.) I found her sitting on a little stool, trying to make sense of the file cards spread out over her bed. She hated to admit she was overwhelmed, but she was. She and I didn't dwell on it then, but in subsequent conversations with each of her daughters, Mom announced her decision not to send a card. "I can wish people a Merry Christmas when I see them."

Giving up the cards was a sign that her memory was fading. She stopped doing deskwork; she didn't keep a calendar any more. She was still holding on, but she was also letting go. Slowly her active, purposeful approach to life began to shift. She seemed content to *be*, more than *do*. She didn't move as fast or remain as socially active. She began using a walker, explaining, "I don't want to fall."

As she became less active, my visits included new ways of making her happy—helping with little decisions, such as selecting which clothes to wear, purchasing stamps, deciding when and how to get rid of all the magazines piled up on her table, which had begun to overwhelm her. There was also the mail: notes from friends but also an ever growing stack of appeals for money for all kinds of causes. Mom was finding it harder and harder to make sensible decisions about which charity to support. Her heart wanted to give to them all: "After all, I am so fortunate." One of my saddest moments was when Mom, who had always balanced her checkbook to the penny and who had caught many bank errors during her lifetime, said to me, "I've lived too long; I can't manage my checkbook anymore." She was ninety-eight.

Mom also welcomed my company in new ways. I'd arrive at her room at the Inn, and there she'd be, sitting, waiting for my knock and entry. She'd clap her hands like a little girl, and then I'd sit across from her, look right at her, and speak carefully so she could read my lips.

My life had changed over the years as well. I had retired from teaching in 1994, earned a Master of Divinity degree in 2003, and worked as a hospice chaplain until 2009. Our own children, Tim and Emily, and our grandchildren, Colin, Jemma,

Clement, and Abigail, were healthy, purposeful, and independent. I had started traveling by myself and loving it. Jim worked from home, gardened, and played golf. I loved our home, but I was restless to get away once in a while. We were comfortable, each following our bliss, which included coming together and being apart. It worked for us.

As I traveled alone, I discovered that I loved solitude. Not just an hour or two here and there but days on end. When I retired from my hospice job, I intentionally accepted fewer obligations to fill my calendar. For the winter months I rented a cottage by the sea off the coast of Maine, an hour-and-a-half drive from home. I would go for four nights of complete solitude and then return home to Jim, family, friends, and church. Cottage in the winter, travel to Scotland and Italy during the other seasons. A new pattern, a new course for my life, was emerging.

Mom was a given in my life and a wonderful one. We loved being with each other, and I have always believed we brought out the best in each other. I took this loving bond for granted until my first trip to the cottage, in 2009, when I realized how affected I was by her fading away. Until then, I had hardly considered there would be a time that I would be alive without her, that she would die. And what's more, I was about to turn seventy.

And so we began, both of us, a new season, a time of holding on and a time of letting go.

Holding On and Letting Go

So teach us to number our days, that we may
apply our hearts unto wisdom.
—Psalm 90:12

NOVEMBER 1, 2009

Hard to believe that I'll be seventy on December 30. It's taken me a while to live into that truth, but I'm getting there. I'm pretty sure this birthday is the catalyst for the cottage-by-the-sea adventure that's coming up in just fifteen days. Another year of the same old Sudbury life just doesn't appeal. I need a change. I want to wake up every morning and decide what to do, which will definitely include reading, walking, quilting, and praying. So strange, this call to pray for people. As long as I can remember I've always been interested in church and God. I need a radical shift in order to see what this praying is all about *and* try it out; I need time to empty myself of all the chatter, judgments, etc., in order to clear a channel and give it a go.

This restlessness has been growing in me as I've been heading toward seventy, circling seventy as I call it. How do I *be* that age? How can I consider being old with Mom still alive and very much part of my life? I don't feel pulled to another career but toward a quite different way of being. This cottage I've rented for the winter has released a new focus. I'll be there in two weeks.

Also hard to believe that I'm part of four generations of women: I'll be seventy; Mom will be one hundred in May; Emily, forty in May; and Abigail, nine in June. Last time I visited Mom (a two-and-a-half-hour drive) I mentioned the cottage to her but I don't think it registered, nor did she remember, and I doubt I'll bring it up again. Her world is small and immediate now. Sad, because a few years ago she would have listened, tried to understand, and been encouraging.

NOVEMBER 2, 2009
Dear Mom,

Here's a prayer from Ethiopia that I came across. It reminds me of the kind of prayer you like to pray:

"God, you have prepared in peace the path I must follow today. Help me to walk straight on that path. If I speak, remove lies from my lips. If I am hungry, take away from me all complaint. If I have plenty, destroy pride in me. May I go through the day calling on you, you, O Lord, who know no other Lord."

On another topic, isn't the following note I just received from Candi [*staff member at the Inn*] wonderful? "Bobbi, your Mom was truly in the spirit of Halloween last night as she wore a blond wig joyfully!!! Candi"

Looks like you all had a good time. Do you remember years ago when Dad would draw Halloween caricatures of the neighborhood children who came to the house?

Love,
Bobbi

NOVEMBER 3, 2009
I'm still smiling as I picture Mom wearing a wig at the party the other night. It's not like her, at least not that I remember. She *never* role-played, probably because she was comfortable being herself. Yet she was always very social at a party, smiling, listening to everyone, making people feel comfortable. Now that she is pretty much deaf, perhaps being in costume gave her the cover to be the person she is so accustomed to being. With that wig, she could waltz around and smile, which is a lot of what the old folks do at the Inn.

NOVEMBER 11, 2009

I'm wired, excited, guilty, scared, and anxious about my start at the cottage: wired that I have so much to do to get ready; excited for a new place and new ways of being; guilty about leaving Jim, giving up church obligations, and being less available to friends; scared that I'll like it too much and want to be there permanently in some form, that I'll become a hermit, that I'll rock the family boat, that I'll lose my public identity, and that I'll have no persona, no idea of who I am; anxious that I'll realize all I can do is play out being old and thus buy into ageism, that I'll discover that being seventy-plus is old and not much fun, and that there are no alternatives, no meaning. And then there is Mom, holding it all together, or is she holding *me* together? Without question she's the most important person in my life—always has been. She's my foundation for family, faith, and solitude and of course a model of how to circle seventy with grace. Ha! She's now circling one hundred.

NOVEMBER 13, 2009

Here's what I wrote to some women friends about all this: "My desire for solitude is *my* need; I'm not getting away from anything but going toward something."

My plan is to spend the weekdays at the cottage and come home for the weekend. It's only an hour-and-a-half drive so what could be more feasible? I'm sensing that I want to write. Of course I'll have a project; I always have; it's who I am. An idea is beginning to form: letters of inspiration to people—women—in my life as seen through the eyes of a seventy-year-old whose mission is to inspire, affirm, and encourage, a woman who from the minute she was born was inspired, affirmed, and encouraged by her mother—*and whose mother is still doing that.*

NOVEMBER 15, 2009

My first full day at the cottage. "Let the sea roar and all that fills it; the world and those who live in it" (Psalm 98).

I'm hunkered down. The waves are battering the rocks. I can't figure out the tides, but the sea is sure telling me I'm not in control. Last night I read in my 12/06 journal that I wanted to live alone—daunting that I still feel that, but there it is. Also daunting that I want to pray for people.

At the moment, this is what is true for me: (1) I love living alone; (2) I don't want any external obligations, although I accept them for family; (3) my life is some kind of example for women, not just seventy-year-olds but all women (alas, the younger ones will be seventy before they know it); (4) I am called to pray for people; and (5) I still have the job of making Mom happy.

NOVEMBER 22, 2009

Woke up at 4:30 feeling the excitement of the nine-year-old me on a summer's day when I knew there was nothing planned, a day free to explore. Outside I would go, sometimes feeling disappointed that the best part of the day was slipping away even before breakfast. Mom and Dad never intruded on these days. I had the freedom of time, space, and imagination. The space of my bedroom, the yard, and the woods. The entire day to myself to live within my imagination. But more than that, Mom never spied on my activities or asked me what I was doing or thinking. From before I can remember I sensed that she honored my private world, as hers had been when she was a little girl.

NOVEMBER 23, 2009

This is becoming an amazing experience, even though I've been back and forth from cottage to home a couple of times and will be leaving here tomorrow to become immersed in family and Thanksgiving. I can do it—the back and forth, the shifting of gears from solitude to social. I don't want to draw attention to this and have the family worry. One of the "dangers" in going off alone is that it freaks people out—they know they are being excluded from a part of me.

Some of my preoccupation with the guilt of going off by myself has to do with one of my "mother tapes"—"stay by your man," or more to Mom's point, "stay *with* your man." Specifically she meant leave him with plenty of food if you're away for a meal and *don't* go overnight without him. When Tim and Em were born, Mom came to help for four nights, only four. On that fifth morning, there she was, waving goodbye, driving off after breakfast, home to Dad.

Now when I visit her, out comes one of her mantras, one of those phrases she repeats over and over. "Well, I guess Jim is managing without you for supper." *Managing* has become a favorite word. She's accepted my solitary trips because she trusts what I do, but she doesn't understand them, nor would she ever have gone off by herself. She and Dad always traveled together, Dad doing all the planning. Maybe this is why I've put *no* effort into explaining the cottage to her.

DECEMBER 5, 2009

I awoke at 3:00 but stayed in bed, intermittently praying, dreaming, and sleeping for two hours. Later I walked a good four miles to the lighthouse and back, doing my best to be in the moment, see everything anew. I remember in the fall of 1998, starting out on a walk to St. Columba's Bay, on the Isle of Iona, struggling to stay present, just as today. This is difficult for me because my usual way is to anticipate and plan ahead. Being future oriented, I can easily miss smelling the ocean or hearing and seeing the gulls.

Like Mom, I move quickly away from the present and immediately attend to the future. Neither of us looks back much. Few regrets. Truth is, I live the future in the present. I want to get away from that pattern.

Case in point, I follow Mom's pattern of grieving. "Bobbi and I don't cry," Mom once proudly announced. She told Margot that when she started crying after Dad died, she immediately stopped, telling herself that she was being self-pitying. I never cried for Dad when he died [*in 1986, at age eighty-one*]. The last time I recall *really* crying was in his arms fifty years ago. As I say, "Mom and I don't cry."

DECEMBER 6, 2009

It snowed last night so I'll have to shovel. I like the idea that what I have to do up here is for my *essential* living, no frills, just shoveling. Sara Mailtand, in her book *Silence*, claims that she wants to live in silence, to be rich in it; for me, it is solitude I long for. Maitland got rid of all the noises in her life; for me, it is about time alone. I envy her simple house in Scotland. What can I create of my own that gives me the essence of what I crave? What do I crave? To be alone with myself and with God and to reach out to others in need. I'm more independent than most people I know, but maybe we all hide it; maybe independence is everyone's secret, whether we have it or long for it. I think of Mom, very independent, happy with God and helping others, but not a particularly solitary person

DECEMBER 7, 2009

Today is Pearl Harbor Day, which happened twenty-three days before my second birthday. I have no recollection of the event, but I do remember the end of the war, or rather the day the news came that Hitler was dead. I was with Mom on Elm Street. It was toward evening, and someone shouted, "Hitler is dead. He killed himself. He set fire to his house and burned."

And now, here I am, sixty-four years later, sitting in my cottage by the sea, thinking about my grandfather's suicide during the Depression and wondering what impact it had and is still having on Mom, what impact it had on her life and, for that matter, on mine. I wonder whether she made the connection that night when she heard Hitler had committed suicide? It was just fifteen years earlier when the wife of the president of Vassar College arrived at her dorm room with the unexpected news that her father was dead.

But now, as she heads toward her hundredth birthday and the twilight of her life, she seems ready to face it again. Throughout my life she was silent, although not secretive, about the suicide; now she often brings it up when Margot or I visit with her. "You know, my father committed suicide," has become another mantra, and then she goes on with some new embellishment.

I'm not surprised Mom and Mimi didn't talk about my grandfather's death. Freud and Jung were in the midst of their important work in 1931, but the field of psychology and therapy did not come into its own until the 1950s. Mom's way was to wait for someone to bring up a topic; she'd listen and then offer a comment, which was honest, consoling, and full of hope. I doubt she ever asked anyone how they were feeling unless she was inquiring about a physical illness. I have to presume that my grandmother never broached the subject.

This isn't the only way to deal with feelings, but it was Mom's way; it worked for her and for the people in her orbit. Rather than dwell on difficulties, she accepted what was and moved on, keeping herself true to who she was—loving, realistic, hopeful, and maybe most important never a meddler or gossip.

I recall a conversation with Mom sometime after Dad died about therapy and analysis. She didn't see the point in delving into the past, nor did she believe it did much good. "We have to accept things and move on. Life is full of ups and downs." She was speaking from her innate disposition as well as life experience. Although she didn't say so, I believe she talked things out through prayer; God was her therapist.

Yet her comments about her father suggest she still had work to do on it. Margot and I tried to listen and pick up cues just as Mom would have done, but the conversation was never lengthy. "I can't believe he left us," she would say. As she did with everything in her life, she came to terms with her father's death, perhaps by holding on to her own life for so long. She wanted no part in assisted suicide. "It is not up to us to decide how or when we die."

DECEMBER 10, 2009

When I signed up to spend time here at the cottage, one of my hopes was to experience winter along the coast. I wanted to be cozy inside while watching the wild, winter ocean. Well, here I am, sitting on my deck/living room seeing, hearing, and feeling the waves beat upon the rocks less than twenty-five feet from the house. Yesterday the sea and sun were delights to both me and the common eiders. This morning I awoke to wind, rain, fog, and wild waves, and it was only low tide. I took an hour and half to watch the tide come in; the locals say that the waves will be splashing the grass.

DECEMBER 11, 2009

Emily is taking my birthday off from work when we visit after Christmas. This touches me. Mom and Dad never made a big thing of birthdays— a few gifts, a simple party with friends, and a cake, which always seemed an afterthought, baked at the last minute; but now I think of it, Mom always made it from scratch. Cake or not, I knew I was special. And I'll always remember the phone call from Dad on my sixth birthday announcing that Margot had been born. Yes, on my birthday. I've always liked that Margot and I share the same birthday. The only time I remember resenting it was when Mom was too busy with Margot's party to give me a ride to the skating pond where all my high school friends gathered that particular Christmas vacation.

My birthday still gets lost in the shuffle, what with sharing with Margot, Christmas, New Year's, and Jim's and my wedding anniversary [*December 28*], so Emily's taking the day is a special gift.

On our way down [*to Lancaster, PA*] we'll stop to see Mom so she can wish me a happy birthday, although I may have to remind her. She stopped remembering a year ago, at least she didn't telephone me. Margot and I will try to make a plan, but it may not happen this year.

DECEMBER 26, 2009
Joyful Christmas with Tim, Jemma, and Clement; family celebration at Sarah's with a little birthday recognition for Margot and me. During the day, when I find a moment to take a deep breath from all the holiday festivities, I dream of the cottage.

A friend told me that our recent conversation about solitude and finding one's bliss meant a great deal to her, was, as she said, a "peak moment." Seems my going to the cottage gave her permission to do what *she* really needs to do.

DECEMBER 28, 2009
Our forty-sixth wedding anniversary. Very relaxing here at home, just the two of us. Tomorrow we head out to see Mom and visit Emily.

DECEMBER 30, 2009
I feel particularly happy on my seventieth birthday. Before they went to bed Colin, Abigail, and Emily decorated the house with balloons and Happy Birthday signs and left little gifts at the spot where I, the first one up, am now sitting. Emily just came down to feed the cat and brought me a cup of coffee before going back to bed. My birthday morning starts with gratitude and joy, all wrapped in solitude.

Seventy years ago Dad and Mom took a cab from Brooklyn to St. Luke's Hospital, in New York City. As Mom tells the story, on the way Dad asked, "What are you going to name this baby?" Mom's reply, "Well, if it is a girl I'd like to name her Barbara." Times have changed; that sounds so formal—the woman named the girl—and my parents never discussed it until Mom was in labor! I was born at 7:05 p.m.

DECEMBER 31, 2009

This is the official seventieth-birthday message that I'll email to friends over the next few days:

> I feel extremely content with life and grateful
> for all the "tenures" I have received through the
> years. My mom is five months away from her
> hundredth birthday and is still the light of my life.
> My teaching career, divinity degree, and hospice
> work are complete, but many other tenures
> continue—good husband, kids, and grandkids,
> wonderful extended family, many friends,
> involvement in church, opportunities to travel,
> and now a new one—more silence and solitude
> and simplicity at the cottage by the sea I have
> rented this winter, just an hour and a half from
> home. It's taken a little work on my part to get
> ready for this new decade, but I've made it. "Hey,
> Bobs, no choice, so you might as well embrace it."

I find that when I am away from my cottage life, it is difficult to embrace the intensity of the experience. Also, I really need three feet: one foot for solitude, another for family, and still another to accompany Mom and make her happy. As she fades away, I feel I'm being drawn to give her a different kind of support. Our mother-daughter dance has always been a fluid partnership, but now I have to lead. We never told each other our secrets—it wasn't like that. But our understanding and the effect we had on each other, and the way we resonated and brought out the best in each other, was perhaps an unacknowledged secret.

Mom knew how to keep secrets:

> *If someone violates your confidence, you find you don't tell that person much if they are going to blather on. Mimi was a good listener and secret keeper. You could talk to her and she wouldn't tell. That's a good quality, really, because we all meet in life people who we feel are not loyal enough, or they say everything to everybody and that's disappointing, isn't it? You tell them something but that doesn't mean that they're supposed to tell everybody.*

> *Besides keeping a specific secret, Mom didn't talk about people. She wasn't interested in gossip. She would listen to my own story, but when I started speaking negatively about someone, she had a subtle but kind way of stopping me. She just wouldn't get into a he-said-she-said conversation. I remember trying to discuss someone's motives with her and hearing her end the conversation rather quickly by saying, "Well, I don't know about that."*
> *I don't believe Mom ever discussed any of us with friends or acquaintances, or with our siblings. Only affirmations and news was allowed. I hold this as one of Mom's most beautiful gifts.*

JANUARY 3, 2010

I'm so happy—this is just where I want to be—I don't want to be anywhere else.

This morning I feared that the forecast would deter me from setting out. And how I wanted to be here experiencing the storm! I can't picture myself having cottage-by-the-sea time at home. This sounds extremely self-indulgent but there's a catch. From the solitude and all this soul work arises the message to get out there and do something for others. It's one of the best of my mother tapes, and of course the Christian message, which Mom lives with ease. It is just part of her.

Of course this longing for solitude and purpose involves Mom. Coming up on one hundred in May, she is deep into solitude, and I am heading there, mirroring her, as I have all my life. I accepted her model as wife and family member and in doing for others, but unlike Mom, in keeping with my times, I had a career. "When your dad proposed to me, I announced that I was going to quit my job, and I did." That was Mom.

But now, in a sense, neither of us has obligations. I am more tuned in to her because she needs my help in practical ways and as a connector to the real world, specifically the hearing world. For practical purposes she is now deaf. Hmm, I seem to need to keep telling myself that!

JANUARY 4, 2010

It occurred to me this morning that I am creating a lifestyle that will serve me as I live into older age—solitude, silence, simplicity, and service. Mom's basic nature isn't one of solitude, although she has always been content with it. Actually, I doubt she's ever thought about it much. She's not as self-analytic or self-involved—read self-centered—as I am.

When I asked her about this she said, "I don't think about it too much. I just decide that I should do certain things and then I try to do them. Get out, see different people, or invite people in or reach out. But I don't think I have to do it; but I have a kind of pattern I fill. I know I do."

And yet, as she circles one hundred she is definitely into solitude, silence, and service, coupled with a marvelous combination of self-confidence and humility. I'd have to say that she lived her complex life with Dad with simplicity. Being hard of hearing for the past twenty-five years has brought her to silence and solitude, but she isn't alone or lonely, because she always has God with her. Nowadays her service is smiling at people.

Mom lived a marvelous balance of faith and works. Going to church was the public naming of her faith, which then played out in all the ways she lived—doing for others, smiling, a prayerful presence. That pretty much sums her up. She kept her well-worn Bible and devotional readings on her bedside table. We all knew that she read them daily, but I got an insight into their true value when we started taking trips together after Dad died. It was part of her morning and evening routine, which she did her best to carry out no matter where she was.

Growing up I was active in church; church was an essential part of our family life. Jim and I continued that pattern by attending the Unitarian Universalist church when our children were growing up, but when the kids went off to college, we stopped going. However, I found myself thinking and wondering about God and for a while I attended the eight o'clock service at the Episcopal church in town. I studied "A Course in Miracles" and read the Bible and various religious books.

I noticed that I kept telling people about Mom's faith: "My mom is one of the most peaceful people I know; if you could have her faith, you'd take it in an instant." After repeating that often enough, it dawned on me how lucky I was to have such a mom, that I ought to take advantage of it, that maybe I could have that peace too. So one day in the 1990s I made a conscious decision to be a Christian. I read the Bible, I prayed, I started attending church, I did my best to think kind thoughts and do kind deeds, and I watched Mom. Ever so slowly discussions of faith crept into our conversation.

I struggle, however, with humility. Unlike Mom, I want people to know the "good" things I have done; I give myself little public pats on the back. I am humbled when I realize that I have no recollection of Mom telling me about any good deed she did. Her actions were intuitive, mine more calculated.

JANUARY 9, 2010

Today I watched a sliver of a moon arise at 6:09, an hour before the sun joined the race. Each morning the sun rises a little earlier. Spring is coming.

Yesterday I made reservations for Scotland: May 27–June 10. I hope to fly to the Shetland Islands for a few days and then go to Iona. Traveling alone is part of who I am at age seventy.

Like Mom, I love to travel and have done so all my life. Growing up, Mom traveled with her family; then with Dad, who was the tour guide par excellence; after he died, with me as the designated guide. But unlike Mom, I love to travel alone.

JANUARY 13, 2010

I have been back and forth from the cottage—to home, to church, to visit Mom, back to the cottage. Each situation is very involving. I feel that I'm on a seesaw that is bumping up and down too fast and too hard. Right now, especially with the calling of a new pastor at church, it seems I have transported my home office to the cottage and unfortunately carried along some guilt that I'm not visiting all the church people on my list. Yesterday, arriving here about 3:00, I headed to the beach.

Here I am, a healthy seventy-year-old with a mother still living, still in an in-between time in my life, wanting to keep one foot in the active camp that I know, love, and do well but also being led to a more solitary way of being.

JANUARY 22, 2010

Here I sit, completely at ease, watching another incredible and yet usual sunrise, thinking of Margot packing to go on a trip, Alice dealing with Mom's desperate dental situation, Ross working hard at his business, while the earthquake survivors in Haiti have no leisure to contemplate the sun, nothing to pack, no dentist to visit, and no business to pursue. We all sit in the mystery.

I got thinking about how apolitical I am, especially up here where I don't turn on the TV or read a newspaper. Until a year ago Mom read the *New York Times* and watched the PBS *NewsHour*. She was informed and had opinions but seldom talked politics. She didn't like people to talk too much, to go on and on expressing their opinions. Part of that but not all was because she couldn't hear what they were saying and so was out of the conversation. Controlling the topic was one way she kept involved. Yet, lack of hearing or not, Mom was and still is very self-contained and assured of who she is and thus has no need to argue or prove a point.

Mom was never a competitive woman nor gauged her merits in relation to others. She had principles and lived her life accordingly. I don't know anyone with more confidence in who she was, a confidence based on humility. In her own words:

> *I think I've been very fortunate in that I've always had
> a sense of—confidence. I don't think I'm overbearing;
> I don't think I put people off because I come on too
> strong—maybe to some people I have. But that's
> the way I feel. I don't want to apologize; this is me
> and I accept people. I have an upbeat attitude about
> everything. Things are going to improve, or you've got
> a chance of improving yourself or the situation. And
> I think some people seem to be born that way. I think
> that of all of you. I'm always happy to hear from any of
> my children because I never think, "Oh, they're going
> to be telling me some terrible tale." Yes, there's just a
> difference in people. I just feel that might be from birth.*

JANUARY 28, 2010

Throughout the night and into this morning I've been working on how to accept all the good stuff that has come my way throughout my life without feeling guilty or, as the saying goes, sabotaging it. Then I got thinking about my life purpose, which for me has to do with helping others.

Mom believes that "we reap what we sow" and lives with humble confidence in what she sows. Almost every time I see her she mentions how grateful she is. "Every day I thank God for my family, my health, my life I had, and my life now."

When I mentioned to Mom that she didn't seem to resent or blame, she responded:

> *There are so many people who do have to blame. It's true that life is not fair. It's like Alice's two young friends, middle-aged, fiftyish, who discovered this cancer, in both cases. It's very sad. But they and their families have got to just somehow handle it, have to manage.*

Nor can I remember Mom feeling sorry for anyone, although she was full of compassion and would acknowledge when someone was going through a tough time. She believed that life was composed of ups and downs and that we learn and grow through them all—grow into more loving, caring people. It was her strong-held belief, faith, that people would not remain overwhelmed by their difficulties but could become stronger and more loving because of them.

FEBRUARY 2, 2010

I'm task oriented, happiest when I have a project, always craving a purposeful life view. I'm feeling drawn back to my quilting. If I have Mom's healthy longevity genes, what is my plan for the next thirty years? It has to be more than physical projects, and yet they are part of it.

Again, the questions come up. How do we create meaning in our lives? How do we feel purposeful as we become less physical? Most of the books I've read on the subject don't address this issue well. They talk about physical decline and tell you to exercise and take up a new hobby. I don't believe they are talking about Mom's age group, certainly not about Mom. She doesn't have anything wrong with her other than her lack of hearing, nor does she have a new hobby; yet she feels her life has meaning. It doesn't take much; a smile, a listening presence is enough, and she's proven that she doesn't have to hear a long story to show compassion. I think Mom would agree that our own meaning comes by contributing to others, by giving others meaning. Kind of a chicken-and-egg conundrum and a human longing for God. No question, Mom's meaning is sparked by God.

How we create meaning continues to be one of my most important questions— maybe the most important! Certainly one I ask more often as I get older but one I never asked when I was teaching or going to divinity school or working for hospice. I didn't have time or reason to ponder; I knew I was doing meaningful work. I doubt that Mom ever spent much time wondering about meaning in her life. Perhaps it is a more powerful question for women who have had careers. Mom's life had a seamless flow: from raising children to a gradual empty nest to volunteering in a different way at church to traveling more with Dad to spending time with grandchildren. She never found herself waking up on the first morning of retirement asking what, now, was the meaning in her life.

This isn't to say all my mother's contemporaries felt the same, but how do we really know? We might look at someone's life and judge it incredibly meaningful, but was the meaning really there for her or just in our imagination? Mom had two things going for her, her optimistic disposition and her faith. "If you're feeling a little down, just go out and do something for someone else." Then she and I would talk about how hard that was for some people and how neither of us knew what it felt like to be really depressed. Mom believed and acted on the Christian meaning, which is love. It was simple for her.

"In the beginning was Meaning, and the Meaning was with God, and the Meaning was God." (An interpretation of John 1:1 by John Macquarrier, quoted by James Carroll in Christ Actually: The Son of God for the Secular Age.*) Mom believed that God is love, and so her meaning was love. Simple.*

FEBRUARY 7, 2010
Dear Mom,

I miss you and just loved the time we spent together last week. We had a wonderful chat when I arrived—very us— and a good time at Alice's. How did you like the signs I put on a couple of your outfits indicating what goes together and the days you might wear them? You helped us for so many years and now we're helping you.

Love,
Bobbi

FEBRUARY 12, 2010
Dear Mom,

I've been thinking about Dad. He would be turning one hundred and five on February 20. We all have so many wonderful memories of him. He was a fabulous father, and such an example to all of us. I think of all his projects and hobbies and of course his love of travel. Then there was all he did in the community, specifically encouraging the building of the New Canaan Inn, where you now live, and designing the water garden. I know you think of him often.

I believe that when your time comes, you will be joining him, along with Mimi, Aunt Kath and Uncle Don, and of course your father. I'm laughing as I think of them wondering why you're still down here with us. "Janet doesn't give up easily," they are saying.

Mom, we love having you around, but it's okay if you decide it's time to leave us to be welcomed into God's heavenly embrace. You have given us all the love we could ever want and we are fine on our own.

I don't know what prompted me to write that, but you and I have always been close and honest with each other, and since it has been on my mind, I thought I'd better say it. You are the best mom I could ever have wanted. God's grace abounds between us. I thank God every day for you and for the relationship we have together.

I love you,
Bobbi

Around this time, when I asked Mom if she thought she would see Dad and all the family members who had died before her, she said thoughtfully, "I hope so. We really don't know for certain but I believe I will." She added, "When I think back to when your dad and I met each other, it seems that we had always known each other and been together and yet I realize that I had twenty-four years before that." She was happy alone, but maybe she could also imagine being with him forever.

FEBRUARY 26, 2010

Incredible storm. Unbelievably cold and no heat, which meant no coffee. I left for home at 7:00. Power out all along the route. First available coffee five miles from home.

I can't seem to release this desire to do some art, but I sense I'd rather organize the supplies than do the work. Bought some art supplies. My plan is to try new techniques with my eye toward meditation, perhaps little meditation books on a particular theme.

Mom's craft was knitting, although she never accumulated a stash of yarn. Her yarn and knitting needles, along with gift-wrapping paper, all fit in her bottom bureau drawer. When she visited a yarn store she picked out the yarn for the next baby sweater and was on her way. I never recall her oohing and ahing over the luscious, pastel baby yarn or selecting a new, challenging pattern. She was in and out of the store, package in hand, and immensely satisfied.

This intentional, precise, just-right purchasing was Mom's way. She didn't like to shop, nor did she want anything for herself. Every year she would spend an hour at the local dress shop and come home with two dresses and a skirt, blouse, and sweater outfit, and that, added to what was already in her closet, would be her wardrobe for the year. Something for dressy occasions, another for church, and a third for everyday. She always looked lovely, in large part because of the confident, easy way she walked and of course her smile.

MARCH 1, 2010

I'm back, so grateful for this place. Up at 4:30 this morning, so I'm about ready for a nap. I was awake at 3:30, dozing on and off. That's the way my body always responds. I figure it's about my exuberance; I'm eating healthy, no chemicals, no wine or meds, and I'm finished with my two cups of coffee by 7:30 at the latest.

Gray, rainy day. Sea is medium active. Low tide. No mergansers yet, but a few gulls are checking out the scene. Temp about 34. When I took the garbage out this morning, the blacktop was a tad slippery.

MARCH, 1 2010

Dear Mom,

I came across this quote from Joseph Campbell and thought immediately of you. Isn't it lovely? "Spiritual life is the bouquet, the perfume, the flowering and fulfillment of a human life, not a supernatural virtue imposed on it."

Love,
Bobbi

MARCH 5, 2010

Dear Siblings,

Jim and I arrived in New Canaan by 10:10 this morning, and I left him at the library and headed over to the Inn to pick up Mom and take her to the audiologist.

She was ready to go of course. She had ready a brown paper bag with remaining batteries, plus the boxes for the aids. What a compliant patient she is! Dr. B. took her immediately and had a seat ready for me in the little examining room. He is kind and very patient with her, and I believe loves her and truly wants to do what he can for her. But how many *really* old people does he treat? He speaks with a thick German accent, which I find hard to decipher at times. Can you imagine what that's like for Mom?

Dr. B. told me that Mom has three problems: she's very deaf; the anatomy of her ears is problematic; and her auditory processing is slow. He reiterated that when speaking to her we don't need to shout, but must look right at her and speak *slowly*. Just because she has poor auditory processing doesn't mean we shouldn't talk with her. She needs the stimulation—use-it-or-lose-it kind of thing. Regardless, it seems clear that writing to Mom, especially any plans, is a good way to communicate with her. She can read them over and over, with time to process.

A couple of funny stories. Dr. B. asked Mom what she had for breakfast—a check for hearing and processing I presume. Mom replied—maybe as a cover because she couldn't remember—"Well, what did *you* have for breakfast?" It took him off guard and I think he felt a little embarrassed about admitting he didn't eat any breakfast. I wonder if he felt as if his mother was talking to him. Anyway, it was all in good humor and it made me laugh. Then in the midst of all the computer testing, Mom turned to me, and with a wink said, "Well, it's good that we only have two ears." She makes me grin.

I had a brief chat with Ann about Mom's birthday celebration at the Inn. They want to do something, and we had previously talked about having a drop-in reception for a couple of hours in the afternoon on Saturday the 8th. I told Ann we can talk about it on March 23, when I'm down to take Mom to her next appointment with Dr. B. I thought Alice and I, with Mom, could talk with Ann and Candi that morning. I'll arrange the meeting. BTW, Mom likes the idea. Please send me any thoughts about this.

Love,
Bobbi

According to Mom, her grandfather had a hearing loss:

> *Gramps tried everything that came on the market to help people hear but he didn't feel any of them did much good. But he had a good sense of humor, and he said that he probably missed a lot of trivia—I don't think that's a word he used—but that if somebody had something important to tell you, they'd make a point of your hearing it. So he heard the important things.*

Mom's hearing difficulty has kept me on a personal and public mission. Because I'm aware that hearing loss keeps us from most kinds of socializing, I have my hearing checked every two years. Thankfully I don't have the ear canal structure that caused much of Mom's problem, but nevertheless, I'm ready for hearing aids at the first indication of need. Evidently, the initial adjustment to hearing aids is easier when the loss is slight. Unlike glasses, which instantly improve vision, hearing aids don't offer the same guarantee of success. They are hard to adjust to our particular hearing needs and are a challenge to insert correctly, fine-tune, and get used to. "Get them early and you'll continue to benefit as hearing declines" is what I hear!

For years Mom had difficulty hearing at church—a jabbering baby, people not talking clearly into the microphone, anything was an obstacle. The only blame game she ever played was around this: the minister's voice was too soft, too low; people mumbled. Her biggest general complaint, however, was that people talked too much. One day when we were discussing her hearing problem, she told me she didn't want to keep asking what, and soon after that she started fading out of the mainstream of conversation into which she never returned.

MARCH 9, 2010

I am back at the cottage. The weather is fabulous and should be all week. With daylight saving time this coming weekend, sunrise will start an hour later again, about 7:00, and the light will linger for an evening walk. The window on the deck is a mess, streaked with salt water, so that is my housekeeping chore for today. But mainly I'm going to follow a book and do some exercises in painting with acrylics. It's time to begin.

I'm also getting this thought that after the age of seventy I can live just as I want—well, within reason—but I'm thinking eccentric, self-centered, reaping what I have sown. It's a different way of being, a different mindset. I want to live a different way in my being. Savor and simplify.

My Scotland plans are coming along—Shetland Islands and Iona.

MARCH 11, 2010

Dear Mom,

I'm laughing because when I send you an email via Candi, I just write "For Mom" in the subject line, forgetting that there are other moms where you're living. But you're the only one for me, and you're the only mom about to be one hundred. Isn't that terrific?

I'm sending you "Blessing at Year's End," by Howard

Thurman. I know that it is just the beginning of spring, but his words of remembrance and gratitude can be prayed at any time. Our family has so many blessings that are worth recalling.

Love,
Bobbi

MARCH 17, 2010

Dear Mom,

Isn't it beautiful today? Warm and sunny.

I'm coming down next week to take you to Dr. B.'s so he can make any adjustment to your new hearing aid. The appointment is at 11:30 on Tuesday. However, I'm planning to come on Monday, in time to have supper with you at the Inn. I'll probably arrive during happy hour, probably closer to 5:30. I'll find you there. We'll be able to chat that evening and the next morning.

Before we go to your appointment I'm going to meet with Candi, Norma, and Barbara to plan your hundredth birthday celebration at the Inn. If Alice can make it, she'll come too. This is a major event for everyone, most of all you , so of course you are welcome to join us. However, you may want to think about what you'd like and talk with Candi about it before our meeting.

Your three girls thought that we might invite people to drop in to wish you a happy birthday and enjoy punch and some cake on the afternoon of the 8th, say from 3:00 to 5:00. We will need to send some invitations so when I'm with you next Tuesday, maybe we can work on a list. I wonder if you have the list of the people you invited to your ninetieth? We will do the addressing.

I love daylight saving time, and *I love you*. See you soon.
Bobbi

MARCH 20, 2010

Dear Siblings,

I had a successful visit with Mom, arriving at the end of happy hour on Monday. She had hosted her sewing group and was pleased with how it went. We had supper at the Inn and then, before I was dismissed at 7:30, we talked about her birthday party.

In the morning Candi, Norma, Barbara, Ann, and I met and came up with some very easy but exciting plans for the celebration, which will be at the Inn from 3:00 to 5:00 on the 7th. As you may know, the St. Marks Fair is on the 8th, making the traffic and parking impossible on the actual day.

Then to Dr. B., who cleaned her ears and her hearing aids, and told her to come back in six weeks so he can clean them again. I didn't make the appointment. She isn't putting the hearing aids in. I think she may be done with them.

On the way home Mom admitted she is discouraged about her teeth and said she hoped something could be done about them. Once again I told her there was nothing the dentist could do, short of major work over many weeks and multiple visits. I think she's beginning to understand.

Candi and Toni [*an aide*] are going to try to check Mom's room more often, but you know Mom. Help arrives at her door and with a smile, she says, "Thank you, I don't need any help today." What can they do? Force their way in?

Love,
Bobbi

MARCH 31, 2010

Dear Mom,

Can you believe this weather? We've had enough rain for a year. But things will improve tomorrow, and Easter should be warm. I wonder if you're going to the Maundy Thursday service at church?

Today would have been Mimi's birthday. How old would she have been? I think of her often and have such wonderful memories of times spent with her, both in Brooklyn and New Canaan. I recall walking with her at a *very* fast pace up Fifth Avenue to buy school clothes at Best & Co. and then having lunch at Schrafft's—BLT and a chocolate soda with vanilla ice cream. I still can't understand why I couldn't have both a soda and an ice cream sundae. And then of course, there was all the Brooklyn Dodgers baseball fun.

I know you have happy memories of your mother, too. She was a good mother to you, and you have been a good mother to all of us.

Your hundredth birthday plans are coming along. Alice, Margot, and I are have great fun planning it together. We keep Ross [*in Portland, Oregon*] informed.

I'm thinking of coming to see you on April 15. I'll let you know the details closer to the time.

Lots of love,
Bobbi

According to Mom, "Mimi was a good mother, and yet she also did outside things. She was a volunteer. I know she was president of the Woman's Federation; she helped at the YWCA in Brooklyn and at church, that kind of thing."

My mother's volunteer work was very important to her and somehow to all of us. It was one way she showed us that we create meaning in our life by helping others. I recall the day she announced, "I have decided to volunteer at the Norwalk Hospital. I've been thinking about it quite a while, and now I believe I have the time to do it." So every Wednesday morning for the next twenty-five years Mom would make breakfast wearing her light turquoise uniform and volunteer pin. "I'm a people person," she would say as she went off to take the money at the café, push the sundries cart throughout the units, or hold the newborns as the parents prepared to go home. When she stopped driving, a fellow volunteer gave her a ride. And then one day she told me she was considering giving up the job. "It's hard for me to walk around; now it's time for the younger people to take over." When she retired, she was given a special farewell at the annual volunteer dinner, and she loved it. Mom was able to give gratitude, but she was also willing to receive it.

APRIL 5, 2010

Sunrise service at our house. The spirit was there for those who got up early and walked up the hill, but due to clouds and trees, no sun. I drove up here after church and sat in the sun on the front lawn, sketching and reading. Such privacy. Then I walked to the beach, which was filled with people enjoying their first sun of the season. Got me thinking that it was time for me to get out of here—too many people, too crowded.

APRIL 9, 2010

Dear Mom,

What summerlike weather we have had, but now it's cooling off and quite cloudy. I'm sure it will be beautiful on your birthday, which is just a month away. What an accomplishment, Mom. You're a trooper. Alice, Margot, and I are having such fun planning your party.

I am planning to come down to see you on Thursday, April 22. If you want, I can take you to the Waveny fundraiser that night, or we can just be together. Whatever you decide is fine with me, and you can decide last minute. You might want to talk with Candi about the plans. I'm going to arrive at 2:30 to chat with Ann about the party and will see you at 3:30.

We had a lovely Easter. The sunrise service was in our yard, with fifteen people and one dog attending; the deacons put on a breakfast at the church after that. At 10:00 there was a joyful Easter service with communion by intinction, which made cleanup for us deacons much easier than when we pass those little cups. Variety is good. Tim and family came for part of the weekend, and Sarah, Per, and the kids came for the first cookout of the season.

See you in two weeks, but we'll talk before that.
I love you,
Bobbi

APRIL 10, 2010

I went outside this morning to see the almost new moon, low clouds, and then all that blue! I was distracted by it all as I flitted from idea to idea, task to task. It's the way I am, but there are times when it doesn't serve me. I found myself tearing up about the power of life, my life and its richness, and loving Mom and knowing she is fading.

APRIL 15, 2010

Dear Mom,

Isn't that great that Ross and Cindy are going to make it to your birthday celebration? It will be fabulous to have all four of us together with you. They are arriving Thursday night and returning to Portland on Monday.

There are lots of plans in the making. When I see you next Thursday the 22nd, I will go over them with you so you can make some decisions, and then I'll write them down for you to review later. One thing you can look forward to is a visit from Debby Cornwell. She is coming to Alice's for lunch on the 8th.

I'm looking forward to a nice evening with you. I'll have to be off before breakfast on Friday.

I love you,
Bobbi

APRIL 23, 2010

Dear Family,

I just returned from New Canaan. Grammy and I had

dinner at Alice and Dave's, which is always so pleasant. Thanks, A. & D.! Mom is doing remarkably well and is even allowing us to help her a little more. Alice has most of the responsibility for watching out for her, which is a huge undertaking and which she does so well. And of course, Margot, Ross, and I all give her the title Hostess with the Mostess, which she takes on with such grace whenever one of us lands in New Canaan. Thanks, A., for being the best oldest sister in the world.

APRIL 25, 2010

Everything is getting set for Mom's birthday celebration at the Inn, where we figure about a hundred people will gather. Ann is putting together a video presentation of pictures from Mom's life, and Candi is making a huge card for everyone to sign. Norma is making the cake.

In the evening we'll be at the Jennings, just the family, about thirty-two people. All eleven grandchildren, minus Kristin, and all eleven great-grands. Alice is doing a fabulous job. I suggested pizza but, no, it will be sit-down with roast beef served on good china. And of course, linen napkins.

At the fifth annual Women of Wisdom Dinner, on May 5, along with other ladies in their eighties and beyond, the church is honoring Mom. I'll probably make a quick trip down for that and then come back with Jim for the birthday parties.

MAY 4, 2010

Dear Bobbi,

Yesterday Mom's sewing group had a plum tree planted in her honor on the hill by the Inn. They all came over after a birthday party at Nippy Eason's, with cake and balloons and cards, taking pictures of her with them in front of the tree, it was toooo cute. She smiled and was gracious and tried not to smile with her mouth open which was v. dear. It was pouring rain when I arrived, but just as they all got out of cars to take pictures, the rain stopped. See you all soon, looking forward, and we probably won't be able to stop the rain forecast for Sat. See you tomorrow, Bobbi.

Alice

MAY 5, 2010

Hi, Bobbi,

I had a lovely visit with your mom yesterday. I reminded her that we are ever available to help as she moves beyond one hundred!! We talked about the church dinner, Women of Wisdom. Then I asked for her "wisdom" about life for us younger ones! We agreed on spirituality, faith, church, community, family, helping others, volunteering, kindness, love, and carpe diem!!!

She will be sharing a little story at the urging of the minister. She has decided to let go of volunteer responsibilities on that Friday at Waveny!

She really is an extraordinary woman. See you Friday!

XO,

Candi

MAY 10, 2010

Dear Mom,

What a wonderful birthday celebration. You must know that you are well loved by so many different people who have come to know you: family, long-time friends, the sewing group, the Inn, volunteer organizations, the church. I could go on and on about each one, but I have to get going with my day, so this note will be quick.

Ross and Cindy are having breakfast with you now, as I write, and then they will be off and heading home to Portland. You have many cards to read, and memories to fill your heart.

Jim and I will be coming by on Thursday, May 20, for

lunch on our way to Lancaster to celebrate Emily's fortieth birthday. I can't believe I have a daughter turning that age! What a delight she is. And you have a daughter age seventy. What a surprise. Another hard one to believe. And then there is Abigail, almost nine. Four generations of women!

I love you, Mom,
Bobbi

MAY 11, 2010
Here is the summary I sent to friends:

> My mom's hundredth birthday celebration was a 100 percent success. And with it, a marvelous Mother's Day for me, with four generations together, which includes four generations of women. Tim and Emily and their kids were there at the hotel, running around with my sister's grandkids. Many festivities, with twenty-seven family members present at Alice's for lunch and supper on Saturday. Over a hundred people attended the party at the Inn for Mom's friends. The weekend ended with most of the family, ages five to one hundred, going to church with Mom and witnessing what church, and this one in particular, means to her. The minister read a short piece describing all the ways that Mom and Dad had participated in the church through the sixty-eight years that she has been a member.

MAY 12, 2010
The family's participation with Mom in church was the highlight of the weekend, at least for me. I'm sure Mom was grateful, but daily events don't make a lasting impression on her these days. All a vague memory as her world becomes

smaller and smaller. Very likely the next time her children, grandchildren, and great-grandchildren gather at the church will be at her memorial service.

MAY 17, 2010

I guess I'm still in disequilibrium about being in my seventies, about how I want to spend my life, what I want to do, and not do, each day. Today I want to be a hermit. Today I want to live in a cottage on the Isle of Skye. Today I know that my all is focused on Mom. How can I know what I want to be when I grow up when I still have a mother? To be an extrovert or an introvert? That is my question. For most of my life I've played in both arenas, but in this post-seventy period, I don't want to do more of the same. I'm sensing it's time for a big shift. I want a more solitary or shall I say introverted life. Clearly time at the cottage is not complete. Hope I'll be able to rent again next year.

Finally, at age seventy-five, I have figured out how, not what, I want to be now that I am grown up. Mom didn't keep me a child, but all the while she was alive I wanted to hold on to the myriad benefits I experienced by her physical presence and by spending time with her. I never wished her out of my life. Not even during those last years, when she was fading away and needing more care, did I ever want her to leave. I was grown up enough then, but now I am living a different kind of grown life, which has more to do with being in my seventies than not having a mother. I am content with my life of solitude and sociability, of traveling and staying home, of personal interests and outreach to others. That was more or less how Mom was, and so I accept it as one of her gifts to me.

MAY 21, 2010

I had a short visit with Mom. She seems to be living on a high about her birthday. So many cards. We looked at some of them, took a short walk, and had lunch before Jim and I started out for Emily's.

The helpers at the Inn told me that Mom hadn't done her laundry, so when I got to her room I asked if she wanted me to help, particularly to change her bed. "No, I'll do it tomorrow." Then Alice came in, and with a fair amount of anger, Mom blurted out, "You girls come and try to take control of my life to the point where I feel I've lived too long because I can't do anything."

We backed off, but oh so sad. So unlike Mom, but I don't blame her. I feel that the people at the Inn are on top of this enough for Mom to function, although it might not be our idea of how she should be doing things. It's a tough call, but as far as I'm concerned, I want to honor Mom's dignity and sense of self and independence as much as possible. I'm also aware that I'm not there with the everyday responsibilities that Alice, living in the same town, on the same road no less, has. I'm reminded of a three-year-old: "I can do it myself." If I live long enough I will come to that too. Good to bring it up with Tim and Emily now, before that reality.

MAY 26, 2010

Dear Mom,

I tried to call you yesterday but you must have been socializing. I'll try today from the airport. As you know, I'm off to Scotland for one of my trips. I'm excited to be going way up north to the Shetlands, and then to Iona and Edinburgh. I recall the fun we had in Edinburgh taking one of those sight-seeing busses all over the city. Then back in 1956 I remember going to the Military Tattoo Festival at the castle with you, Dad, and Alice. Aren't memories wonderful? We have the best of them.

Love,
Bobbi

MAY 27, 2010

It's clear to me that my days talking with Mom on the phone are over. I'm not certain she hears the ring right away, and when she does answer, she can't hear and she gets confused because so many are unsolicited calls—which she resents and doesn't understand. We're alike on that one! That isn't just an age thing.

MAY 30, 2010

Easy flights: Boston, Philly, Glasgow, and then on to the Shetlands. It was a long day, but I've caught up with my sleep. Yesterday I took a boat ride around the Isles of Bressay and Noss, and saw literally thousands of gannets nesting in the high cliffs. Today, another tour, to Clikimin Broch and to the Isle of Mousa. Tomorrow I'm doing a self-guided tour of some Iron Age ruins, only a short bus ride from here. I love public transportation!

The weather has been fantastic, with plenty of sun. So far north there are no trees. I can see for miles. What a trip. I'm so happy traveling alone. This aloneness always leads me to new dimensions. I feel released to accept this and not feel I have to share what cannot be shared or to feel guilty for the fullness of it.

JUNE 1, 2010

Am at the café at the Lerwick airport waiting for my flight to Glasgow. I've loved my time in Shetland. Never a sad moment, but I'm hardly ever sad. Although it's been a touristy time and I've been more chatty than usual, my underlying theme, my search for meaning, is always with me. What is my purpose at age seventy? Right now I feel some envy toward two young women chatting about their lives at a table nearby. I don't envy their particular issues, but the time and possibilities of adventure they have ahead of them. I've had a great deal of adventure in my life, but I want more—or do I? I want something different, but what? Active purpose has to be different at this age. Reason: could be health, but also a different view of the future, with limits of years ahead.

Immersion in a craft still excites me but so does doing nothing; visiting, but also being solitary. At the moment, this is what I know: (1) I don't want many different facets in my life; I don't want to wake up every morning with piles of responsibilities and a long or even a short list of things I have to accomplish; (2) I want to live for the day, aware that things will change; (3) I want whatever I choose to be possible even if my health or life situation changes; (4) I want to make a difference in people's lives.

I doubt that Mom ever made that kind of list, but she would resonate with number 4, making a difference.

Mom found making a difference was rooted in faith:

> *I think that what people do with their time and energy shows what they really believe. Maybe they don't want to discuss the dogma or beliefs so much, but I think they feel why they are here. Why are we here in life? Well, we're here to help other people. I have the feeling that if I'm so fortunate to have good health and good eyesight, a lot of things that people my age don't have, I should be giving something back to other people or helping those people who are less fortunate. I think that's part of the reason I keep busy volunteering at the hospital. I like to do that, and seeing people who can't get out and do things. I like to go call on them and take them something.*

JUNE 3, 2010

This place [*Iona*] exudes peace. Getting here is a challenge, which makes the serenity of the place more palatable: flight to Glasgow Airport, bus into the city, bus to Oban, spend the night there; next day, ferry to Craignure on Mull, bus across Mull to Finnphort, ferry to Iona. And then all the chatter in my head goes poof, right up to heaven. A simple life. Ah, simple is the word I'm searching for. No other human being to argue/disagree or even agree with; nothing I have to do. Doing takes the form of being here on the island. Iona is called "the thin place"—that liminal place where heaven and earth meet. That's all I want to feel.

From my 1996 journal, the first time I came to Iona:

> *I walk along, the wind gently breathing upon a hovering medley of clouds. Stopping along the gravel road, lined on either side by sheep, I startle myself by saying out loud, perhaps to those sheep or to myself, perhaps to the universe or to God, "Life is simple; all we need to do is to love each other." For the moment I am standing in the "thin place," that liminal space between heaven and earth, between time and eternity. I am in the presence of God.*

JUNE 3, 2010
Dear Mom,

I was so sorry to hear from Alice that you had a fall on Sunday and had to go to the hospital. Now you're home and on the mend, but I wish I could come down and be with you. On the other hand, you have good care where you are.

I am on Iona now for five days before going to Edinburgh; it is beautiful and sunny, which isn't always the case in Scotland, as you well know. You and I never came here together, but you and Dad wandered the island as part of a daytrip from a cruise around the British Isles.

Love,
Bobbi

JUNE 4, 2010

Dear Mom,

Greetings again from Iona, my second full day on the island. Today it is windy with sun, clouds, sun, and on it goes. I've breakfasted and am sitting in the sunroom of my hotel overlooking Mull and watching the ferry go back and forth. I'm glad I walked to St. Columba's Bay yesterday while the wind and sun were steady. Today I'll stay close to home and take a tour of the abbey, something I've done so many times before but I'm always ready to learn anew.

Love,
Bobbi

JUNE 5, 2010

Today was sterling. I climbed Dun I, the tallest mountain on Iona, all three hundred and thirty-six feet, and stayed for three hours, sitting, reading, writing, looking, being, and even napping in one of the rock crevices. I thought of Alice O. Howell and *The Dove and the Stone,* a love story about her visit here with her husband Walter. I thought of my childhood and how happy I was playing by myself and with a few close friends. I thought of how Mom always honored my play and made sure I had time for solitude. I thought of this call to pray for people and the spark of God's love that I've always been aware of in me, a spark from God, passed on to me through Mom. Then I returned to the hotel and took a luxurious bath.

JUNE 8, 2010

On the bus from Oban to Glasgow, before taking the train to Edinburgh, I mentioned to the woman sitting beside me that I quilted. "Oh, that is very powerful work. Women's work, meditation and with their hands. People are returning to crafts that are permanent, rather than those that are destroyed or thrown out when not needed anymore."

JUNE 14, 2010

A quick visit to Mom. We did some errands; the bank for a little cash, post office for stamps, and the local pharmacy for lipstick—although she has plenty. Mom stayed in the car while I went into the bank and post office, but when we got to the pharmacy, I got her walker out of the trunk and she moved step by step in and out of the awkward entrance and up and down the narrow aisles.

Ever since she stopped driving, these errands have become part of our routine whenever I visit. It's a welcome addition, giving us something to do, as conversation has become limited. Mom and I used to sit and talk for hours, but over the past couple of years that has faded and now is almost bleached out. We are holding on in new ways.

On this visit, as she often does, Mom mentioned that she missed driving but that she was glad she made the choice to stop when she did.

I still smile when I remember how it happened. She had just celebrated her ninety-fifth birthday and had announced that when her insurance ran out at the end June, she was going to stop. It was so like Mom to get her money's worth, even those last two months of car insurance! After all, what a waste not to use it! I don't think she ever considered asking for a refund. It wasn't her way to return something she had purchased. A deal was a deal.

So there she was driving a short distance over the New Canaan line into Stamford for her yearly checkup with her optometrist. She knew the way well. When she walked in late—Mom was never late— she announced to everyone in the office that she had been in a little accident but, "It wasn't my fault." She had hit a man on a bicycle, but he wasn't hurt; she knew the way, but because there was a detour she had gone down a one-way street the wrong way. But it wasn't her fault. Her optometrist checked her eyes—excellent. The secretary offered to drive her back to the Inn, but Mom said, "No thank you, I know the way," and off she went. As soon as she arrived at the Inn, she told the story again, and Candi immediately called Alice and me. We never needed to tell Mom that it was time for her to stop driving. She beat us to it that very evening. Done. Decisive Mom.

The next day she called her local garage and sold the car to one of the mechanics. What a deal! That same day Dave followed her there; she handed over the keys, paid a rather large bill for work they had just completed on the car, and picked up the check for the sale. That was that. As I say, what a deal and what a mom. She made a decision, acted on it, and never looked back.

A few days later Dave went to the police to inquire about the man Mom said she had hit and to learn what had happened. The story is sketchy. The man was okay, it was just a graze; he let it go. Evidently Mom had pulled to the side, but never got out of the car; she must have smiled her way through whatever the policeman said. We're pretty sure she didn't understand any of the details. How could she with her lack of hearing? I wonder if he told her she could go or if she just decided that the conversation was over and so off she went.

One postscript. Under normal circumstances, Mom's car hardly needed to be serviced; she probably drove no more than ten miles a week. The engine, however, got a workout every time she started it up, because the only way she knew the car had started was to rev the engine. While in neutral she'd press the accelerator until she heard and felt that all was ready. Then she'd back out and off she'd go.

JULY 1, 2010

So glad I visited Mom again before all the comings and goings at Camp Fisher. She was her lovely, peaceful self. Full of wisdom. She sat down a lot. Needs to be alone. I sense a shift. I told her of the joy of Emily and Tony's upcoming marriage, in our back yard on the 4th, but I'm not certain how much of it registered.

JULY 3, 2010

All is going well with the festivities. I've stopped trying so hard to clean up and keep things tidy. Of course, it's getting done, although not always at my pace. I realize that the young people have different tastes, interests, and knowledge than I do, and different standards of order and neatness. I don't always have to be in the flow, like I'm their age. An ongoing process. I can't believe that I'm just realizing this, but then I've never grown up quickly. I still think I'm a kid, and very likely I'll always feel that. After all, I have a mother! I remember Mom stepping out of the fray and letting the young take over. Go, Mom, go, me!

I have continued to step back and let Tim and Em be the new grown-ups in the family. Although I still have the physical energy, I don't want or need to be mentally and emotionally as involved with all the details. They can set up the aero beds, bring in the firewood, go to the grocery store, and cook a meal. Our grandkids are now in their teens, so we're not needed to watch them nor play with them as we used to, which is a little sad but of course in the order of the way life goes. Jim and I are grateful that we can still be part of their lives and are beginning to echo Mom's comment, "I'm glad I've lived long enough to know my grandchildren as adults."

JULY 5, 2010

The wedding was marvelous. All that we had hope for or imagined. This feels like a new beginning for me. Emily is happy, and Mom is tucked away for me to visit. When everyone leaves and the weekend is put away, I'll have two weeks to myself to quilt, visit, and tend to my prayer/spiritual life.

I'm feeling more settled about being seventy—but not yet completely there. Maybe I never will be, since I've always thought of myself as childlike. I looked young, matured late, and lived in my imaginary world while my school friends were playing at being grown up. During my junior high school years I straddled two worlds: school, where I pretended to be an adolescent, and home, where play had free rein. That secret life was where I was most my true self. My bedroom (including my closet), the woods behind my house, and the dogwood tree in the front yard were my havens. I was at my happiest alone in my own worlds, and I believe that is still true. Mom knew this about me and without saying anything, or telling anyone, she gave me the space to figure it out and live into it. She still honors my independence.

JULY 15, 2010
Mom was her usual self today, doing her best to keep going, make decisions, stay independent. The nurse came in and took her blood pressure: 112/62. Not bad for age one hundred! Not bad for anyone! If Mom could give her blood pressure to someone younger, she would.

Once again she brought up her father, remembering him in such loving ways. Again she mentioned the difficult circumstance surrounding his death and the Great Depression. "Of course we are in a somewhat similar time now, people losing jobs or not having one that uses their talents." This lady is still with it!

I feel sad for Mom, especially since my self-appointed job has always been to make her happy. Here I am, happiest when I am alone, and Mom missing her father. I wonder if all of this is connected.

JULY 17, 2010
Why am I happiest when I am alone? All my childhood memories include some kind of solitude, most of them of times I was playing alone, outside or in my room. Even when I was with friends and family, the essential memory is of being alone in the presence of others.

My dolls and teddy bears were an essential part of my life growing up, way into junior high. I learned through play, which may be the reason I chose to teach kindergarten and why play became an essential part of my curriculum. I have the dolls Mom played with. "I loved dolls. I always had dolls. I took care of them. I also liked paper dolls a little bit later. I could set up a little room or house on the floor, and it was the dollhouse or paper dollhouse. I had them conversing."

AUGUST 11, 2010

I showed a therapist friend the little note Mom sent me last week. She was amazed at the coherent message *and* the handwriting. "This is a lady who has her mental faculties and who has a positive outlook." In handwriting, a steady hand indicates no dementia; letters slanting to the right indicate a positive disposition and attitude toward life.

My friend acknowledged that this is the message *everyone* longs for, the mom everyone wants. In some form or other we all ask, "Does my mother love me?" We all want to feel a resounding yes in our heart. Although the question gets answered in our early years, we keep asking, we keep pondering. Mother love is a life force. Mine is a powerfully good one.

AUGUST 12, 2010

Visited Mom yesterday. Came home mentally exhausted and sad. She seems so alone. Lonely? I don't know. Waiting? Yes, but wanting to lead a productive life right to the end. I'm sad because I can't visit her every day. I want to make her happy. That's been my job since I was three, and I want to keep doing it.

We had an interesting discussion about her teeth. She started by saying that she wanted to see the dentist so she could get them fixed and ended by "deciding" that she'd have to live with her teeth just as they are. She mentioned that Alice said it would be too expensive, and I added that the procedure would take many visits, be painful, and take a lot out of her. She went over and over her decision and decided that she could give up eating corn on the cob but that thankfully she can still enjoy coffee ice cream, a brownie and a glass of milk, and her nightly happy-hour glass of Cinzano. She agreed that she wanted to enjoy her life until the end. "Some things you just have to accept. Now that I've decided, I don't have to talk about it anymore."

I want Mom to live forever, but I feel a little down about her plight. She's trying so damn hard to keep going and has so little to look forward to. I wish I could pop in every day. I think I'll start sending her little scripture readings and prayers. It also helps her when I put in writing memories from the past, as well as what we just talked about.

AUGUST 13, 2010
Dear Mom,

It was wonderful to spend the morning and eat lunch with you yesterday. Weren't we lucky to take a walk in that nice cool air? I think you made an excellent decision not to have anything done to your teeth other than cleaning. As you said, aside from the expense, it would take many visits to the dentist and would be very painful. Having teeth pulled takes a lot out of one's entire system. You may not be able to enjoy corn on the cob, but you can keep up your addiction as a chocoholic and enjoy ice cream and brownies, and still enjoy a glass of Cinzano during happy hour.

As I think about this, I realize that you have made excellent decisions throughout your life. *Picking Dad as a husband was your best.* Five years after he died you decided when to move from Wahackme Road and then, ten years later, from Hatfield Mews to the Inn. You knew when to give up driving, and now, to have no fancy dental work. You are remarkable. Always decisive.

I'm glad that a lot of your thoughts these days are about Dad, for of course they are pleasant. He was a wonderful husband and father and a friend to many. I believe that when the time comes, you will be joining him, Mimi, your dad, Kath, and Don. It's a mystery of things hoped for, dimly seen now but seen in full later.

I love you, Mom,

Bobbi

AUGUST 15, 2010

Dear Mom,

I sure am lucky that you are my mom. You're the best. I wish I could take a walk with you today, even in the rain. We could carry an umbrella.

Love,

Bobbi

Mom was not athletic, although the early movies Dad took around the time I was born show her biking and sailing. I remember Mom buzzing around the house at a fast and determined clip, and walking to the mailbox. When she moved to her condo, she developed a daily walking routine down Kimberly Place. She had to cross a main road to get there, and aware that she couldn't hear, she'd always stop and carefully look both ways at least two times. By the time she moved to the Inn, at age ninety, she became even more adamant about walking every day, and this became part of our routine whenever I visited. We'd walk up Oenoke Ridge to the Roger Sherman Inn, where we would tap the sign, turn around, and retrace our steps.

When Mom started using a walker, probably after she gave up driving, she would stop along the sidewalk, pick up trash, and stash it in the pocket. Back at the Inn she would empty the bits of paper, Styrofoam cups, beer and soda cans, and even banana peels into the wastebasket in the lobby. "I just wonder what the people's homes are like if they throw coffee containers out the car window?" became another mantra. Alice's friends would comment that they saw Mom doing her civic duty. It was suggested that Mom join an "adopt-a-street" program.

AUGUST 18, 2010
Dear Mom,

I've had a quiet week, although Tuesday I drove my friend Edie to her chemo appointment in Boston. She was diagnosed with ovarian cancer five years ago, and things are beginning to take a downward turn. Very sad, but she is remarkable in her faith and willingness to share and be open to living each day fully.

Off for a picnic with a friend—that is, if it doesn't rain. Hope you are continuing to be able to say, "I am well." Your spirit lifts the spirit of others. On the other hand, it's okay if you have some down time. You have a great support system at the Inn to help you—Candi, Ann, Delia, Barbara, Toni, Francis, Alva, and Pino, plus Alice of course, always available, always wanting to do what is best for you. You're lucky to have a least one daughter so close by. You know that I wish I could drop in every day. I wish I were with you today, your laundry day, to help you change the sheets on your bed. *Carpe diem.*

I love you,
Bobbi

SEPTEMBER 1, 2010
This house *feels* like it's a mess. I ought to throw stuff away and sort through the piles and files. But there's always something more interesting to do. I go through this every once in a while, this angst and urge to purge. Maybe I'll gear myself up to take a day and just do it. That is, after Italy. I'm very ready for this trip. When I travel, I am in the moment.

SEPTEMBER 3, 2010

Mom had just finished exercise class when I arrived to visit. We went to her room, where she immediately sat down and watched me change her bed, asking a couple of times if she could help me. Then out of the blue she blurted, "I have someone who comes and does my laundry all the way from Boston." I couldn't tell if she was joking or stating the truth as she saw it, or maybe somewhere in between. I got her sheets, towels, and several changes of clothing into the washing machine and the aide, bless her heart, said she'd finish them up. I mentioned to her that Mom was a little quiet today and she said, "Yes, sad." Francis cuts through it all to see the essence of things, to notice the joy and sadness in a person. She loves Mom, but then she is not her daughter so the love can be simple.

Mom has stopped getting her laundry basket from her storage area in the basement, and before that, when she was still driving, from the trunk of her car where she kept it. She no longer puts up her heavy, *very old*, ironing board to fold her laundry on. She used to iron *everything*, even Dad's boxer shorts, but that is long past. She has always been such a creature of habit and routine; it makes me sad to see so much of this fading away.

We are hoping that the church can find someone to give her a ride on Sundays. Calling a taxi is definitely not a good solution. Nor should Alice have the responsibility. She feels awkward about this, but she does so much for Mom and needs her Sunday mornings free, to go to church or to stay home. We are grappling with the same issues at MCC. A good challenge for churches: they ought to be committed to find ways to get all the folks to church who want to go, especially the older ones who don't drive anymore. Local families do enough without that added burden.

SEPTEMBER 5, 2010

I'm debating whether I should cancel my trip to Italy but have decided to go forward unless I hear of some major Mom down turn in the next day or so. There's going to be a time when I may want to stay close by, even in her room, but although that could happen any moment, the time isn't yet. And then, maybe Mom will die in her sleep while I'm away. To quote another of her mantras, which she applies to many situations, not just death, "We're not in charge." Of course this is how I want Mom to go. Or do I?

Mom wants no part of euthanasia. Take care of yourself, keep living, and do good—that purpose again. It's God's call, not yours. It's part of her faith, but also I think it has to do with her father's death. As she once told me when we were talking about some friends of hers who at the end of their lives chose assisted suicide: "Well, it's very hard on the family." Mom wasn't one to elaborate or talk on and on about it. She got right to the point. How could I forget?

Also, strange as it seems, I think of this trip to Italy as a gift from Mom, a letting go of me, as I let go of her. It will help me be free. Reminds me of leaving home for my junior year of college [*in Florence, 1959–60*]. It was my first time letting go of family, and now it feels like my last time, at least of letting go of Mom, although she has never held on to me. Am I talking about letting go psychologically or leaving physically? Probably both.

Walking alone around Florence will give me some time and space to sort stuff out, and let Mom go, or perhaps experience a sense of life without her. Of course there will be memories of all the trips she and I took there after Dad died.

SEPTEMBER 7, 2010

Dear Mom,

I'm off to Italy. Remember when I went for my junior year in college? You were so encouraging. That was just three years after you, Dad, Alice, and I took that fabulous trip from Italy to Scotland. And then there were our trips together after Dad died: to Scotland, the land of our ancestors, and to Florence, the city of my heart and I believe yours too.

You have been a fabulous mother to all of us, and you still are. The good thing is that all of us are doing well and can cope on our own. You've always been grateful for that. Also, we have one another. The work of your job as a mom is done. Now all you need to do is smile and think of seeing Dad sometime soon.

I love you,
Bobbi

SEPTEMBER 10, 2010

I am finally here and settling in, in body/mind/spirit. I want to write in this journal, for it is where I will reread and remember. I'm not quite ready to begin the task of writing seriously again, but it's coming back. Journal writing may be where I'll begin.

SEPTEMBER 14, 2010

I've ordered wine at a café in Fiesole overlooking Florence. I can pick out all the buildings, and of course the Duomo, which overpowers. Its awesomeness could be frightening, but for me the entire building is an anchor and a scaffold. What do I mean by that? I'll have to sit with the thought. All I know right now is that it has been and still is a symbol of who I am and a harbinger of more to come. Something about my independence and mettle to follow my bliss.

Sipping the wine makes me think of Mom, who came here to this very place with me. Way back in 1982, I showed Mom and Dad how to get here on Bus 7. I'm not a poet, but here's one for Mom:

This is my time, Mom, to say goodbye to you.
The Fiesoli bell is boldly ringing you home.
Bold as your life has been,
Bold as your parting.
You rang every moment,
Your gift to us.

SEPTEMBER 16, 2010

I spent the morning with hundreds of sixteenth- and seven-teenth-century paintings at the Pitti Palace. Now I'm enjoying a huge salad at Piazza Spirito. There are few places for privacy in Florence. A woman is sitting near me having a glass of wine. She opens a notebook. What is her story? Does she write in a journal like me?

I remember receiving a red five-year diary with a lock and key for Christmas when I was in grade school; I was loyal to it for about a month. I have the journal from my first trip to Europe, with my parents in 1956, and from my junior year of college, in Florence in 1959–60. But it wasn't until the 1980s that I became a consistent journal writer; the first one I can pull off the shelf is dated 1982.

If and when anyone decides to read these journals, they are going to be mighty bored. No gossip, no personal opinions about family. Just pages and pages all about me. If anything, they will conclude that I was one of the most self-involved people they ever knew. You see, I journal to figure things out—my life purpose, my teaching, my faith, and my mom as she began to age. It is most startling to realize that if I hadn't, this book would not exist, at least not in this form.

SEPTEMBER 19, 2010

Yesterday I walked along the Tiber from Trastevere to St. Peter's and then took a bus back to the hotel. I was at odds all day—fragmented, sad. The overt sadness of age seventy hasn't been with me lately but it lingers still, and there it was as I walked.

Today is different; I'm back in harmony, in balance. What shifted? Yesterday I was scattered, not knowing where to go. Today I got going and loved the *now*; stayed in the moment. At the end of the day I wrote a few emails. I'm facing homeward, getting ready to do some visits after all this time just for me. This call to do for others is strong, not for attention and accolades but for my heart. Getting ready to be with Mom.

SEPTEMBER 20, 2010

A friend has started a blog. I've been intrigued by the thought of writing one ever since I first heard about them toward the end of my teaching days. But, I wonder—is this another idea I won't follow through? If I choose to write one, I think it will be about finding meaning in our seventies. Worth considering, worth planning. Worth a draft.

Title: *Circling Seventy, Finding Meaning*

Purpose: There is a new generation of women heading toward seventy or moving on from it. We are healthy and have been successful in our lives, with careers of worth. Some of us have raised families and now we have grandchildren; some of us are caring for aging parents. We don't want another career, but we want to be useful in the world, we want our life to have meaning, we want purpose. Some of us haven't eased into this effortlessly. We can't believe we are seventy.

SEPTEMBER 21, 2010

As I type away here in Rome, I have a luscious cup of espresso before me. I'm wondering if a lifestyle of time at home, interspersed with solitary trips and days at the cottage, will become my new pattern of responding to a more simple and less social life. Maybe a blog would keep me connected in a new way, while Mom is still here and after she's gone.

SEPTEMBER 24, 2010
Dear Mom,

Do you remember those 16 mm movies Dad took when we were little? Well, I had them put onto a DVD, which I'll bring for us to look at. They are wonderful movies of you and Alice, a few of me as a baby, Aunt Bow, Uncle Don, Kerrin and Donnie, Mimi and Aunt Kath, and even your grandparents and Dad's father. The scenes are from Shelter Island and Brooklyn. In every one of them you have a welcoming smile. You still do.

Mom, it will be wonderful to see you. It's been a month, which is way too long. As you know from my postcards and email, I had a wonderful time in Italy. Visited so many of our favorite haunts.

Love,
Bobbi

What impresses me about these movie clips is how easy Mom is with her smile and how comfortable she is in her body. She is both business-like and effortless in her demeanor. Very honest, no pretenses. There she is fishing and laughing about it, same with riding a bike—each moment full of joy, too natural to be a one-time appearance. Yet I never remember her fishing or biking or even expressing an interest.

OCTOBER 1, 2010
Mom's world is getting smaller and smaller but she is still her lovely self. She takes that one thyroid pill every other day. She is in no pain—no nerve endings?—but has an enlarged aorta that will send her off one of these days (or years). She is one of the most peaceful people I've ever known, but no denying, it is strange to be seventy years old and have a mother, especially one who still mothers me in the best way ever. How can I grow up? Why would I want to?

Reading over what I've just written, I realize that many times in this journal I mention that I am seventy and still have a mother and then review who Mom is and what she means to me. I seem to need to hear it again, write it again, experience it again.

OCTOBER 2, 2010

The blog is coming along; for now I'm naming it *Circling Seventy*. It feels so right to be immersed in something; computer communication and reaching out to others is what I love. I like quilting but don't want to do it night and day, and besides it involves getting out, keeping out, and putting away too much stuff. With a blog, all I need is my computer. Simple.

The project offers a huge learning curve. Right now I'm looking at blog designs—and figuring out how they work for readers—and writing text. This may just be my next tenure project—I'm at my best when I have one. The bottom line is that I seem to be able to inspire, affirm, and encourage people to follow their bliss; I have to believe there are many out there who would like to communicate about this and take their first step. My life seems to be an example that tweaks others to create their own life of meaning.

OCTOBER 4, 2010

Dear Mom,

Here is a beautiful thought from the poet Rumi:

The heart is nothing but the
Sea of Light . . .
the place of the vision of God.

Love,
Bobbi

OCTOBER 9, 2010

A year ago I wrote about my fears in going off to the cottage by myself. I talked of letting go of my public persona. Thankfully

I'm in a more healthy mood about it now; it's not an either-or situation anymore. To disappear from society would be to die, and I'm not ready to do that yet. I have something to offer others and myself. Also I don't fear the truth that I am happiest alone, something I've expressed, not implied, to those who count— Jim, Tim, and Emily. That's a truth that needs to be proclaimed!

Mom has always known that she had something to offer others. It's her nature. I wonder if she's still feeling that. It's hard to tell, but again she told me that she could still smile at people. As far as being alone, that's not her true nature but she has settled into it as older people do—through physical limitations and a natural, normal process of letting go. That's what I observe. And yet, Mom is still holding on. It's also worth noting that although meals are provided, she is still living pretty independently at the Inn. They carry out their mission well,

> . . . to provide you with a caring and supportive environment that helps you to maintain your independence, enjoy a carefree lifestyle, and live life to its fullest.
>
> Our staff is dedicated to promoting your independence, wellness, dignity, and choice. We provide numerous amenities and will greet you by name and treat you with the warmth and respect you deserve.

OCTOBER 10, 2010

Yesterday I ended up rushing about with and for Mom. I clearly needed more time with her and yet she dismissed me after a short visit. Her sense of time is going. Wish I could whip in and out every day. Must definitely go every two weeks. And yet she is doing well. She seemed to like the video of Alice and me as toddlers—didn't fall asleep, watched the whole thing, but didn't show much affect. She gets confused about the days of the week, and it doesn't help that part of the Sunday *New York Times* arrives on Saturday. She reads "Sunday" and so thinks that that's the day. She doesn't want anyone to help her, which can be a problem. When an aide comes to her door, Mom opens it, smiles, and says, "Thank you, but I don't need any help today." What can they do? Certainly not barge in. Really rather humorous.

Am thinking hard about why I feel so energized about the blog *and* the cottage. With these two actions in my life, present both now and in the future, I feel connected to my Self. I'm alive at the moment, but even if this were my last, I'd be at peace. Content in the moment. I feel at one with God, with the mystery. Life is fine now and for the future.

Particularly, three pieces are in place: the cottage gives me personal freedom and independence; the blog gives me outreach and intimacy; family, friends, and church offer aliveness between the two. Without the blog I might feel like an old woman with no purpose, going nowhere. I have to believe that it will be of value to women—and men—circling seventy in figuring out their particular purpose behind the bigger purpose of life. The purpose behind the purpose.

Mom has figured out the purpose behind the purpose, although she probably can't articulate it. Explaining it has never been her way. She's always had a natural knowing about it. But she's there now, sensing it in her being, which is enough. Clearly she's both holding on and letting go, but still I wish she would life forever.

OCTOBER 11, 2010
Dear Mom,

Please don't feel badly that you sometimes get mixed up about your schedule. At age one hundred you have permission to be confused once in a while. You're doing so well staying independent and making most decisions for yourself.

But it is okay to need some help. One decision that you can make for yourself, however, is whether it is worth wearing your hearing aids.

Tomorrow is your wedding anniversary. How many? You married the right man, that's for sure. I know you have many happy memories of your life with your dear husband and our fabulous father. I believe that he is waiting to be reunited with you when your time comes. What a hopeful mystery we live in.

I love you lots,
Bobbi

OCTOBER 17, 2010

A thought: restlessness comes when we don't feel challenged or when we feel we're just repeating our life with nothing new. I wonder, do many women feel this restlessness at age seventy? They have completed their public life work—career, volunteering—all the while raising children, running a household, and following hobbies. Now what? Men, notwithstanding changes in child rearing and breadwinning, retire and then start a hobby, almost as another career. *Breadwinning*, now there's an old-fashioned term, one Mom loves.

Edie [*diagnosed with ovarian cancer in 2006*] had a good report. She has taken care of her body and soul. A miracle she calls it. I think miracles are best kept silent. Float the word but don't give the details. After all, by definition, they are unexplainable.

OCTOBER 24, 2010

Numinous thought this morning: human beings all have a holy longing—longing for unity, at-one-ment with the ineffable, union with God, peace of God that passes all understanding. Deep in our souls we ache for peace, which isn't satisfied *out there* but *in here*, inside us, in our soul. Sure, it's easier to feel peace when we have food on the table and when we like ourselves, and yes, our projects and careers *do* matter. But that deep experience is within. I think of Mom, just sitting there in God's presence, waiting for me to arrive. That *holy longing* is satisfied within her in her aging.

OCTOBER 29, 2010

Stopped to see Mom on the way to Emily's. It takes Mom all she has to keep track of her routine. Evidently the other day she got confused about the time and came down dressed for church in the middle of the night. She remembers fewer family members.

Blog is coming along but I think it's going to be about solitude, not about circling seventy.

NOVEMBER 4, 2010

I made incredible progress on my blog yesterday. Settled on the site provider. Current working title: *A Cottage by the Sea*, for people who sometimes want to be alone.

Rereading last year's journal I notice that I have resolved two personal issues. (1) I was concerned about telling people about the cottage. Well, now they know. As far as I know they accept it, but really, I don't care what they think—well, not very much. (2) I was searching for a purpose in the form of a project. Now I have it.

NOVEMBER 9, 2010

Mom is really failing. She can't remember what day or time it is and she isn't eating properly. Is that a problem? Having no teeth doesn't help but part of the problem may be that she thinks eating chocolate is nutritious. And then all the physical mechanisms of swallowing and digesting are shutting down. Makes me sad for her. My sadness is that I don't know if she is sad, happy, lonely, you name it, although I do sense that sometimes she is aware that she is confused. That is *not* Mom. She's always been thoughtful and intentional about her life. Confused is an adjective no one would ever apply to her. My lifetime job to make her happy is changing, but it's still there. I just want to be right with her, whatever that might look like. I'll be glad to check things out on Thursday.

NOVEMBER 12, 2010

Arm in arm, Mom and I watched the Veterans Day flag-raising ceremony at the Inn. A beautiful moment. She took it all in but didn't say much and was pretty silent as we took a drive around town. The only topic she brought up was Italy and how she loved all our trips there.

NOVEMBER 20, 2010

Today I launched the blog: *A Cottage by the Sea*, a blog for those who like silence, solitude, and simplicity and who sometimes like to be alone.

NOVEMBER 23, 2010

I'll be heading home about one o'clock today, picking up the turkey on the way. I'm geared up to pull out my extroverted self and give everyone a good Thanksgiving, me included. The blog continues to be fun and to feel right—a call to reach out, to offer kindness, and walk humbly. It is grounding me, giving purpose, which strangely enough finds me less self-involved— well, less wallowing in purposelessness.

I want to understand what Mom is trying so hard to do at this twilight time in her life. Why she is holding on? She is rapidly losing her sense of time and place; she is well taken care of and still smiles God's love, but she can't let go.

NOVEMBER 23, 2010

Via email I've told some of my friends about the blog *and* about this idea that sometimes I want to be alone. They were enthusiastic and delighted that I could work out my cottage plan—but come to think of it, that's how friends are supposed to respond. Most said that they liked time alone and felt it was important. Some said they had their own cottage-by-the-sea time; most wanted more time alone than their situation and busy lives could manage. A few said they had too much time by themselves.

NOVEMBER 26, 2010

The house is full of people and clutter—as it should be. Grandparents, parents, grandchildren—as it should be.

DECEMBER 6, 2010

Church with Mom was fabulous—the music, the sermon. But the best part was the Call to Worship and Prayer of Confession, which Mom participated in. She was always three or four words behind the rest of the congregation, so when we were finished with a section, she was still reading, for all to hear. Evidently the minister and congregation have learned to wait and then continue. It was a beautiful moment.

DECEMBER 7, 2010

Dear Mom,

I loved being with you yesterday. Going to church was so special, mainly because we were together, but also because of the service. The music was spectacular, as was Skip's [*Harold Masback*] sermon. I also appreciated meeting Chris Delmar, the new pastoral care minister, who told me she plans to visit you and others at the Inn this week. I'll have to come back to visit another Sunday, perhaps in January.

Brunch at the Inn was delicious and full of good fellowship. I enjoyed sitting with some of your friends and was thrilled to learn that one of them once lived in the house we rented on Oenoke Ridge when we first moved to New Canaan. I have many memories of ages two to six when we lived there, before moving to Wahackme Road.

Mom, I know that you think a great deal about your wonderful father. It is a mystery why he had to take his life the way he did; and it is difficult to understand that he left his wife and family. But I believe that Mimi knew he loved her and that you still know he loved you. I'm glad you can talk about this. You and I are such optimists that it is difficult for us to put ourselves in others' place when they are depressed.

Stay warm. You are the best mom in the world for me.

I love you,

Bobbi

DECEMBER 12, 2010

Mom fell yesterday. Alice whipped over and got her up so they didn't have to call 911 and send her to the hospital. I'm grateful for Alice, who will go back tomorrow morning to check on things. Strange as it may sound, we all agree that Mom doesn't need to go to the doctor. What for? She's not in pain, and she's one hundred. It's so good that Alice got there in time before they had to call an ambulance. Even though Mom has a do-not-resuscitate order, they'd have to run a bunch of tests. Institutions have to act like institutions, hospitals like hospitals. How profound!

It seems that Mom knows it is important for her to get out and about, attend things, pass the time productively. Living in the present and not giving up is deep within her. So today, since she didn't have to spend the time in the hospital, she went to church, had lunch at the Inn, returned to church for Lessons and Carols, and then attended her book group meeting. She doesn't read the books anymore, but evidently she always makes a comment that cuts to the heart of things. She's been part of this intergenerational group since soon after Dad died. They all love her presence and participation—a kind of "friends of Janet" attitude. The other blessing, along with Alice, is that the helpers at the Inn love Mom and will do anything for her. Same helpers have been there forever. Great stability of staff.

DECEMBER 13, 2010

I don't always want silence. I certainly didn't yesterday afternoon at the *Messiah* Sing. How can one listen to the "The Trumpet Shall Sound" and "Hallelujah" in silence? Well, maybe Beethoven. He was deaf when he wrote the Ninth Symphony and then went on to conduct its premier. But that's not to assume that being deaf was his first choice. And for those of us who don't compose music, we want two ears that hear.

Mom doesn't want silence either, but I might as well face it, for all intents and purposes, she is deaf. Her hearing aids don't help anymore, so she has given up fussing with them or even putting them in. All the same, yesterday she went to Lessons and Carols. She follows the program and I bet she can think the tunes. I love imagining Mom and Beethoven making music in silence.

DECEMBER 20, 2010

Mom fell again, and this time they couldn't get her up, so here she is at the hospital; I came down to be with her.

I remember sitting in the hospital feeling Mom slipping away from me. She seemed pain free, was friendly and accommodating. She smiled but she didn't make much sense. Instead of conversing, as we had done a few years before during another hospital visit, I was there to be her ears, eyes, and voice, explaining to her what was going on, translating her intentions and desires to hospital personnel, and navigating the medical system so that she could get out as soon as possible and spend her remaining days in a comfortable, homey. and safe place.

As Mom was letting go of her life, I had no choice but to let it go as well, this life I had known and loved for over seventy years. My job to make her happy now took center stage, never had it been more important and obvious to me. Mom couldn't advocate for her physical needs, and, like everyone, she deserved a peaceful, happy end.

DECEMBER 20, 2010
The Mom Report
[Monday morning]
Dear Siblings,

I arrived here in Room 805 about 7:30. Mom was awake, looking so beautiful. Shift was changing, people were introducing themselves, Mom was smiling and I kept saying to everyone who came in, "She can't hear," that is until I told myself to shut up. More later.

[Afternoon]

The silence, solitude, and simplicity that I brought from the cottage is holding me in good stead as I sit with Mom, waiting for everyone to figure out the next best plan for her. She lives in the silence of deafness and has always created the solitude that she needs. At the moment her voiced choice is simple: "I want to go back to where I live."

I'm learning about silence, solitude, and simplicity through the situations of others. I've been here twenty-four hours gathering stories. My humble conclusion is that everyone, yes everyone, is trying to make sense of their lives, hoping for meaning, as they keep going.

To begin with, there is the woman who cleans the floors. She came here ten years ago with her husband and *one* of her children, leaving most of her family behind. "But it's okay," she tells me, "and I will get back there someday."

Then there is the man across the hall, waiting to be released so he can go back to the shelter where he lives. He's eating a good lunch first. "It's going to be cold," he's told.

What about the aide who is going to New Jersey to see an aunt after work? *She has her own life.* I am once again amazed to realize how involved I have become in my immediate situation, only to grasp how true it is for everyone else.

And then there's the little Italian woman, walking the hall, getting ready to go home. She stops and I listen to her entire story. My choice. I could have withdrawn into my own silence. But not to worry, it's there for me whenever I want it. Which reminds me to stay very grateful.

Love,
Bobbi

DECEMBER 21, 2010
The Mom Report
[*Tuesday morning*]
Dear Family,

Some of you are aware of what's going on but I thought I'd write it up and send it along to the whole family before the day begins. As Mom said yesterday, "We sometimes don't know what's going to happen next. We just have to wait and be patient." And so she is, waiting at the Norwalk Hospital to "hear" when and where she's going. It will be to Waveny, a skilled nursing facility affiliated with the New Canaan Inn where she has been living for the past ten years, and she seems content with that, but only as an interim stop before returning "home."

I wish you could see how cute she is, winking at everybody, although she told me that she is getting too much help for her liking. Ann and Alba came by to visit, bringing Mom a plant and some candy to eat before supper. They love her and can't bear the thought that she might never return to the Inn.

[*Later*]

Every once in a while Mom starts to get out of bed. She points to the closet and says she going to get dressed and go to church. I tell her that she can't go now; she complies and gets back under the covers. A little later we repeat the pattern.

Everyone here is trying to figure out what's wrong with her. Maybe nothing, but that is too countercultural as far as hospitals and old ladies are concerned. Unfathomable. Nothing wrong? Sure doesn't fit any pattern in the medical world. They have monitored her heart and the doctor just reported that Mom has aortic valve stenosis, mild to moderate, so her fall probably was not caused by her heart. What?

We're leaving the hospital with *no* meds. No surprise!

Love,

Bobbi

For all intents and purposes, Mom was never sick. I remember once Dad telling us that was she in bed with a cold; what gloom in the house. The next day she was up and about. Mom rarely took a pain-killer, even a few years ago when she felt arthritis in her hands and knee. She silently weathered it, occasionally grimacing when getting up from a chair. We didn't talk about it much, but one day I asked her how her knee was feeling. "Oh, that pain is all gone." And so it was.

Growing up it was not much fun to be sick. Sick enough to stay home from school, you must be sick enough to stay in bed! Mom would bring us juice and a toasted cheese sandwich; she would fluff up our covers and check in periodically, but she didn't stay to entertain us. We were sick.

As a parent, I continued this no nonsense approach. My kids didn't like it much at the time, but I notice they are continuing the pattern with their own children. I know that genes play a part, but being sick has never been fun in my family. Same with painkillers. We don't take many. I am grateful for Mom's wellness message.

DECEMBER 22, 2010
The Mom Report

[*Wednesday, early morning*]

Dear Siblings,

The bottom line is that as of last night Mom is at Waveny, and so delighted to be there. She is already queen of the place, chatting with people and waving at everyone she recognizes. She owns the place as far as she is concerned and still believes she is an active volunteer there. What a transformation. Her extrovertedness and lightheartedness were so apparent. Wish you all could witness this, but more than that I wish you could be with her, and she with you.

On the way from the hospital she told me that all her children were good drivers; by the time we crossed the Norwalk–New Canaan line, she was talking about how little time it had taken us to get here from Sudbury. When I left her last night she was holding court about how she had gone to Massachusetts to visit me and then had a quick stop at the hospital. I wonder if the hospital is fading from her consciousness? "Good idea, Mom, dwell on the positive." Isn't that so like Mom.

Love,

Bobbi

[*Wednesday evening*]

Dear Siblings,

This morning when I got to Waveny about 9:30 Mom was sitting in a wheelchair in her room waiting for a physical therapy evaluation. She seemed rather sad and listless, the antithesis of last night's elation.

Alice and I talked with the admissions people. They plan to have a case meeting about her next Tuesday—Alice and I, *and* Mom, will attend. At that time they hope to have a sense of what's best for her. Can she return to the Inn? Would she need help and how much? Would it be best to stay at Waveny or go to a less expensive nursing facility? The cost is the same, whether the stay is temporary or permanent. If she were to remain at Waveny she would be in the same room; nothing would really change.

We have much to process. None of us receive all the information firsthand, so it is important that we ask questions and make our thoughts known to one another. We're all in this together, although clearly Alice has the bulk of the work and on a daily basis as well.

Love,
Bobbi

DECEMBER 23, 2010

Oh, my goodness, it just occurred to me that I spent the past three nights in Mom's bed at the Inn. She is hoping to get back there, but I think she'll get used to Waveny and like all the help she is getting and truly needs.

I've been an emotional extrovert these past days. Nothing silent about it. Good to be home and preparing for Christmas.

DECEMBER 28, 2010

Jim and I had a very satisfying forty-seventh wedding anniversary yesterday with Tim and Emily, Colin, Jemma, Clement, and Abigail, at Tim's.

Mom is in my heart all the time. I wish I could be with her more, just to hold hands. But she is fine—I know that. The decision has been made: she will be living at Waveny. They have her using her walker because she was forgetting to put the brake on the wheelchair. When asked about staying at Waveny, she said, "I don't want to be a burden to anyone. I'd like to be at the Inn, but I like it here." This was at the end of the meeting, most of which she slept through. We have until January 26 to clear out her room. I'm hoping that Alice, Margot, and I can do that together.

DECEMBER 29, 2010

Today I'm thinking about silence. You'd think it would be simple: to me silence is no external sound. But it certainly isn't simple when I think about Mom at age one hundred living with no sound because she is deaf. Her thoughts aren't silent, however, even though they don't make any noise.

When she was born, in 1910, Alexander Graham Bell had already held the first telephone patent for thirty-four years. I don't know when her family first got a phone in Brooklyn, but I do know that when we moved to Connecticut we were given the number 9491; later we had to add a 9 to the number; next was 966-9491; and finally the 203 area code was added. How many calls were sent and received over the years through that number? How many plans? How many secrets? And now with Mom moving to an assisted living facility, the number the family held for sixty-nine years is being disconnected. I presume that 9491 will arbitrarily be assigned to another family, but for our purposes the number has vanished except for the memories of things spoken and listened to after dialing it, and maybe, just maybe, those conversations are still floating around in space. Life goes on.

DECEMBER 30, 2010

Dear Mom,

Can you believe that today Margot and I are celebrating another birthday? Age sixty-five and seventy-one, respectively. How could you have been so clever as to give birth to two children on the same day? When I was younger I didn't always like sharing my birthday with my little sister, but now I think it is wonderful. Good job, Mom.

Emily, Tony, Colin, and Abigail are here. Emily, Abigail, and I are going to a *Sound of Music* singalong. Em is dressing up as Maria, Abigail as Gretel, and I will wear my long black coat with hood and be a nun. Tonight Emily and Tony are cooking me a surprise birthday dinner. "Surprise" in that I don't know the menu.

You are a brave soul, Mom. I know you were hoping to return to the Inn, but it seems best for you to live at Waveny and get the help you need. You know many of the people there and you are in the town that you've lived for almost seventy years, so that is a good thing. Your smile will bring joy to all the people there. I will come down in about ten days to see you.

I love you lots,
Bobbi

JANUARY 6, 2011

Dear Mom,

I know that you are warm and cozy at Waveny. It is a beautiful spot, and the view from your room is idyllic.

Yesterday was my last official deacon's meeting at church. I've had the "job" for six years, so it's time for a change all around.

Margot and I are coming down to see you next Monday. She hasn't seen where you are now living. She will love it.

Today is January 6, Epiphany, so I've copied Matthew 2: 1–12 for you to read. I'll always remember your response when someone asked you your favorite book. Without hesitation you said, "The Bible. I know it well."

See you in a few days.
I love you, Mom,
Bobbi

JANUARY 9, 2011

Alice, Margot, and I are meeting with the team at Waveny tomorrow at 10:00. We will learn more about Mom's status and care, but we also have the opportunity to express *our* status and the care we want for her. How to convey that we are ready for her to go without sounding ungrateful or selfish?

After all, we are aware that it is "all about Mom." In some regard I feel that Mom is holding on not only to her life but to us as well.

It will be cathartic for the three of us to express our deep feelings, the socially acceptable ones and the shadow ones, in front of one another and the others.

JANUARY 11, 2011

Storm alert. We're going to finish clearing out Mom's room this morning. I'll visit her and then head to the cottage. It's all gone well. The three of us have had a lot of laughs, shared memories, and worked hard. I haven't wanted to take much of anything, which has made it freeing and easy, a sign that I am into simplicity. I did, however, take three things: Dad's paintings that I had "loaned" to Mom when she moved from her condo; Mom's typewriter, on which she had typed every check she ever wrote; and Mom's letters and files. She sure saved a lot of papers! The most precious treasure is the file boxes and index cards.

I don't think Mom knows that we are clearing out her room. We haven't told her; it would just confuse her. She has a lot of memory loss and cognitive gaps. She seems content but mentions that she'd like to go back to the Inn. Then in the next breath she says she likes the help she gets. "I told my helper not to leave me."

The three of us had a successful meeting with the folks at Waveny. It is clear that Mom needs 24/7 help, which wouldn't work for her at the Inn. This is the best place for her.

Last night I sat with her during happy hour while she sipped her doctor-prescribed Cinzano and I, a ginger ale. She asked me again about my trip to Italy and how Jim got along without me, and then reviewed her father's death. I wonder if the memory of his apparent suicide is keeping her from letting go, with "don't leave me" being part of it.

JANUARY 12, 2011

I was mentally and physically exhausted last night when I finally arrived here at the cottage. Turned out the light at 8.50 and didn't get up until I turned on the coffee at 5:40. Now I am mentally and physically delighted to be here with two full days alone, although I have some church emailing to take care of as I plan the reception for a member's memorial service. I want to be silent for a while. I feel called to create my own life with God, call it silence, solitude, and simplicity, with service and prayer. Letting go of Mom's stuff and seeing Mom now in her essence are the signs that I have to let go and move on.

All we have here is snow. I can't even see across the bay. It's fabulous.

JANUARY 13, 2011

Following the solitary path isn't easy; even putting that first step forward is a challenge. There is so much to give up and *that* brings forth sadness; giving up a lifetime of parental/societal training comes to mind. "This is the life you *should* lead: be nice, be polite, conform, don't leave your man, don't rock the boat, follow the straight and narrow." Thankfully Mom offered other training as well, but her life with God was solidly behind her "be nice" message. And *that* is what I don't want to give up. *That* is where it feels I am being led, but it doesn't mean it's easy, letting go.

Mom has always had that deep God place within her, and the essence of her beautiful self is still here to show me the way. Now that she is physically cared for, she can be here as a model of faith.

Maybe the piece she needs to work out is how God fits into her father's death. We all have our own narrative behind asking why bad things happen. It's the Christian/religious story played out over and over again, with suicide an added challenge. I also wonder if Mom will live to spend down her money for her care, thus showing that material possessions are immaterial in the long run. Big lesson there. Possessions have never been important to her and money was to give away, although she was also careful about it. Never one to squander until the last few years, when she wanted to give to every appeal that came in the mail. That's when she had to surrender her checkbook.

JANUARY 14, 2011
Dear Mom,

I loved being with you on Monday and Tuesday. You seemed very peaceful in your new surroundings. Your room has a lovely view, with a gazebo. Remember the one that Papa built at Wahackme Road? And then you and I used to sit and chat in the one at the Inn. Alma is a lovely roommate. And now you are getting the wonderful care you need. You are one fortunate woman.

Here's one of my favorites from Psalm 34: "Take delight in the Lord and he will give you the desires of your heart."

Today I am meeting Janet, your first grandchild, for her birthday lunch.

Love,
Bobbi

JANUARY 20, 2011
Dear Mom,

Well, we certainly are into the weather, aren't we? More snow than last year. Not much news to report from here. I've been doing some writing and have been visiting people from church. Speaking of church, I hope that you can get to yours once the weather improves and the walkways and steps aren't hazardous.

Today I've been thinking of the fruits of the spirit as mentioned in Paul's Letter to the Galatians. I've written them out for you as a reminder, although I know they are deep in your heart. "By contrast, the fruit of the Spirit is love, joy, peace, patience, kindness, generosity, faithfulness, gentleness, and self-control. There is no law against such things." Galatians 6.22–23

I love you,
Bobbi

JANUARY 25, 2011

Although we are all on the same page about Mom, the three of us have some differing concerns about her. At various times one of us says: she needs to get out more, the TV is on too much, she's just sitting, she's hanging on too long. I take the stance that Mom's life is just as it is meant to be. Tom [*my pastor*] emailed me that he is praying that Mom feel the peace of Christ that is encircling her. That's all that matters to me—and that she is physically comfortable. I'll be glad to spend some time with her next week and for a while try to see through *her* eyes and through *God's* eyes, not through a daughter's eyes.

Right up until the end, Mom shared herself generously with her four children. She had no favorites, just different relationships with each of us. She kept up with her eleven grandchildren and cherished their frequent visits, as they did with her. She and her twelve great-grand-children loved smiling together.

JANUARY 26, 2011

Dear Mom,

More snow, but I know you are cozy and warm, and so are Jim and I. I was telling Pastor Tom about you and he said that he would pray that Christ's peace surround you at this time in your life. Isn't that the best prayer?

This morning I came across these familiar scripture readings. I thought you might keep them in your pocketbook and read them from time to time.

"The Lord protects the simple; when I was brought low, he saved me. Return, O my soul, to your rest, for the Lord has dealt bountifully with you." Psalm 116. 6–7

"The Lord bless you and keep you; the Lord make his face to shine upon you, and be gracious to you; the Lord lift up his countenance upon you, and give you peace." Numbers 6.24–26

I'll be seeing you next Tuesday. I can't wait. Hopefully it will be clear so we can take a drive.

I love you,

Bobbi

JANUARY 27, 2011

I'm thinking about the early life lessons I got from Mom. For some unfathomable reason, she and I were always in sync. She understood my childhood ways and thus was just the right mother for me. It wasn't that I could do no wrong in her eyes but that her ways brought out my best. I was her good, easy daughter.

Although it wasn't her way to discipline or reprimand in any obvious way, I remember her doing so once, speaking with clarity as she gave me that "mother look." I must have been ten and she wasn't letting me do something that I wanted. So I told her she was a "dumb bunny." She raised her finger and said, "Don't ever speak to me that way again!" I never did.

We know these early lessons and messages, these early ways we lived in the world, become the foundation of our particular life work. Mom's message to me, one that she still sends as she fades away, is that I'm fine the way I am. I think she received a similar message from her father, which she was able to hold on to in spite of his sudden and horrific death. I also think she passed that on to my siblings, although of course their experience was different.

So now, with Mom heading toward "a good death," I

figure that I should be able to hold on to what she gave me. I sure won't have to deal with the sadness, questioning, deep grieving, that accompanies a tragic end. In her hanging on, and her letting go, Mom is doing everything she can so as not to repeat the past.

JANUARY 31, 2011
The Mom Report
Dear Siblings,

Time with Mom was delightful but quiet. She was sleeping on top of her bed when I arrived, evidently something she does every afternoon. But she woke up, and immediately said "Bobbi." We did quite a bit of smiling and looking at each other before going to tea in the recreation room. Back in her room she read Ross's email and opened some mail. I have the sense that she needs to be helped with that, in that she forgets what to do or even to do it. We also looked at recent photos of the family that are gathered in a little photo book, as well as the picture of her parents in a frame on her bureau. I then walked her to the dining room. She now has her meals where she can get some help and be watched, not in the room where the rehab folks eat. Evidently she isn't eating much, but twice a day is given Ensure as a supplement. I told her I'd be back tomorrow morning, but I doubt that she'll remember.

I think she is "happy" where she is. By happy I mean content in a rather passive way. Not much going on in her mind, which is at rest. I'm reminded of people who practice meditation—empty mind, deep contentment. "This is my home," she told me, and then referred to the Inn as "that other place where I lived." She loves the nurses who tend her and often holds on to them and says, "Don't leave me." I think she feels safe, and how good is that?

Mom has a little chest cough. "I can't seem to get rid of it," she says. Of course, she's had *no* experiences with this kind of thing, having never been sick in her life—well, I only remember one time. I'm going to mention it to her nurse and ask what they might (or might not) do about it. I'll ask that Dr. P. H. be notified so he can listen. What to do? This kind of thing can be a slippery slope, just when we think we have directives in place. We just want her to be comfortable. Along this line, I asked the nurse why Mom didn't have a do-not-resuscitate bracelet. "We don't have the patients wear them here, but we have the paperwork at the desk. We know your wishes." I think they like us and know that we all have Mom's best interests at heart.

Love,
Bobbi

FEBRUARY 1, 2011

What am I to make of the way Mom hardly paid attention to me yesterday? The mom I have had for all these years is fading away. Understandable, sad, very sad for me, and yet I don't feel rejected; I don't think Mom could every make me feel rejected. Maybe unconsciously she is releasing me from the job I have had all my life, which has been to make her happy. I know from my years working in hospice that people make the final journey by themselves. They don't need a family member helping them along, at least not in the usual way. And what's more, we loved ones can't keep hanging on to them. Did Mom release me from my lifelong job? I guess it's up to me to interpret. Maybe it will end up being her final gift to me, but I'll keep visiting and doing what I can to make her happy. I may be released, but I'm going to keep the job, keep on doing it. Maybe not for Mom but for me.

FEBRUARY 2, 2011

The sea is roaring today; yesterday it was calm. I can barely see the lighthouse on the Nubble. Wow, windy out there. The snow is blowing all over the place. We're due for eight to twelve inches. I'm ready for the adventure. I feel a little like I do when I take my solitary trips, excited, on my own, ready for surprises.

Strange how this sense of release from Mom, and my acceptance of it, has made a difference in my attitude. I still feel close to her, but it's like we had this relationship, this love, but now we must let it go so we can stay together. I have a legacy to carry on. I'm on my own in a new way. Although I'm free from my job to make her happy, I'm still going to try. How could I not? I may have a new mental attitude about it, but it's still my job. It's hard wired.

I wonder if in releasing me, Mom is making space for the aides who help her, who can make her happy in the ways she needs right now? Fine with me. Maybe she sees her father in them when she tells them, "Don't leave me."

FEBRUARY 4, 2011
Dear Mom,

I loved being with you on Sunday, and I agree with you that Waveny is a good new home for you. People take care of you, your family and friends can visit, and you have a wonderful roommate and a lovely room with a view. I'll be back to visit in a couple of weeks. If this snow stops, maybe we can take a drive or even get to church.

I love you,

Bobbi

P.S. Did it ever occur to you that the Bible doesn't mention snow? Of course it doesn't. No snow there.

P.S.S. Here's a copy of Psalm 61.

FEBRUARY 14, 2011
The Mom Report
Dear Siblings,

I found Mom in her room, nodding off, but she woke up quickly. I signed her out and off we went on a drive down

Wahackme Road to Hatfield Mews and on to the Inn, where she wanted to visit, and so we did. Everyone who works there was thrilled to see her. We even went into the living room and heard a saxophone quintet practicing. Lovely sound; I presume that in her own way, Mom heard it, too. We got back to Waveny in time for lunch. Mom ate two bites of broccoli, four tortellini, and one slice of canned pear. Just isn't hungry. I figure the only way she's going to die is through starvation. No, let me say through not eating.

She and I had very few conversations and I didn't try. There's nothing in her mind to talk about. However, when Alice came in, she immediately got that A. is worried about Dave [*Alice's husband was in the hospital*].

Love,
Bobbi

FEBRUARY 18, 2011

I continue to be mystified about this being seventy. Can't believe it's happened to me. It came upon me by surprise. Maybe because I still have a mom. I hardly noticed those other decades. I wonder if turning seventy is one of those universal secrets. Not the mechanics and outward changes that one might expect—bodily changes, financial and health concerns—but the secret of how we feel inside about life's meaning at this stage. The first secret is the emptiness, a change in anticipation of the future, a loneliness, a lack of psychic energy, the knowing and feeling that we are truly alone. The second secret is the solution, and if we're lucky we can latch on to it—the longing for and finding of the ineffable, which I name God, which lets us know that we are truly not alone. I believe Mom has a lot of this figured out. But then, she's one hundred.

FEBRUARY 19, 2011

For a while this morning I was the only person on the beach. Later a woman appeared and began collecting things, and all at once I was not alone. I asked her if she had found any treasure, to which she replied, "No, I've just picked up some glass so the children won't cut their feet." Then her voice trailed off, "I guess I'm just a mother." I wanted to shout back and tell her about my mother, one hundred years old, purposeful with her smile, fading away from me, just the most wonderful mother for me. I wanted to tell her how my mom, until just a year ago, was picking up litter along the road. I think this woman would get it.

That deeper solitude that I had experienced earlier on the beach had vanished, and I was back in the social world in my role as a "citizen of the beach." It wasn't until I entered the cottage that I got my solitude back.

FEBRUARY 19, 2011

Dear Mom,

More snow here but it shouldn't last. Not another blizzard, thank goodness. But it is cold. I'm sorry the cold prevented you from going to church yesterday but maybe next week. As you always say, "We're not in control of the weather."

Thinking of you and looking forward to visiting the week after next when Jim and I go to Emily's.

Dad's birthday tomorrow. He would have been one hundred and six.

I think of you every day, Mom, and thank God for you. "I thank my God every time I remember you, constantly praying with joy in every one of my prayers for all of you." Philippians 1:3–5

Love,
Bobbi

FEBRUARY 21, 2011

I launched my prayer blog today: *Aprayerdiary.net*. I feel energized—a similar feeling to when I was involved in the combination of teaching and writing. Now, here I am, living in silence, solitude, and simplicity, and blogging about it; and praying and writing about it. The doing supports the writing, the sharing. Clearly my life works best when all is integrated. Purpose, purpose, purpose, meaning, meaning, meaning, bliss, bliss, bliss. In practical terms, for me it seems to have to do with sharing and writing. Writing is my craft, my art.

FEBRUARY 24, 2011

Dave is now in rehab at Waveny with Mom. She knows he's there but she can't take it all in. God is protecting her from the pain she cannot handle. Mom always agreed with that adage that we are never given more than we can manage.

FEBRUARY 28, 2011

Recently a friend asked me why I love coming to the cottage so much. "What do you experience there that's so special?" I don't have a very adequate response, but I'm working on one. When I arrived here today I had to shovel a little slush before I came out on the porch to enjoy the view—today's wild waves and tomorrow's anticipated sunrise. The shoveling and the view are special. But there's another kind of delight that I can only express in the negative. I have no schedule, no possessions that need tending, no food to prepare, no conversations. There is an emptiness that feels positively peaceful. The specialness lies in simplicity, which balances my thoughts and activities regarding Mom.

MARCH 1, 2011

Dear Mom,

Beautiful day here. Hope it will be the same on Thursday when Jim and I come to see you. We'll be on our way to Emily's.

I understand that Dave has been "with you" at Waveny. I hope that he'll be able to get home soon. He's had quite an ordeal. I'm sure you have enjoyed Gail's visits. See you Thursday.

Love,

Bobbi

P. S. Here is a favorite from Psalm 24: "The earth is the Lord's, and the fullness thereof; the world, and they that dwell therein."

MARCH 4, 2011
The Mom Report

Dear Siblings,

Jim and I arrived at Waveny about 11:00. He went into the library to use their WiFi, and I found Mom in the activities room. Today was baking day; ten or so ladies and one man were sitting around a large table, aprons/bibs on, all participating in making New York cheesecake. Each had a job, and Mom was in the middle of hers when I walked in and sat down. She was using a spatula to take the cream cheese filling off the electric beater. Just the woman for the job. I think every grandchild has a memory of baking with Grammy and anticipating licking the beater and wishing that she had left more batter. But not this woman, who lived through the Depression.

After the cheesecake went into the oven, there was time for the balloon game. For twenty minutes they batted a balloon back and forth to one another. Everyone seemed totally involved, and Mom was right in there playing.

Then it was lunchtime. I bought soup and salad and ate while Mom organized all the things on her tray. She took the plastic wrap off each glass—water, juice, milk, and coffee. It reminded me of the way she organized all the things on her desk back at Wahackme Road. However, aside from a couple of sips of juice, she didn't eat *one* thing, and I don't think she had any intention of doing so. Perhaps she forgot what to do or maybe she wasn't hungry. Evidently she had eaten a "big" breakfast.

Mom seemed glad to see me but didn't mind when we had to leave. She referred to the Inn as "that place where I used to live." When I asked her if she wished she still lived there, she gave an empathic *no*. Said she liked being with the other people, meaning that little cohort of residents who do some cooking activity every day from 11:00–12:00. I think it's just the right little social group for her. Jim came in for a short visit, and then we got off for Emily's.

Love,
Bobbi

MARCH 7, 2011

The way Mom arranged her lunch the other day brought to mind a childhood family ritual known as get-your-own-Sunday-night-supper. It was a somewhat radical idea in the days before takeout and microwaves. At least it deviated from the norm in our house of eating all meals sitting down as a family. My recollection is that every Sunday night I fixed the same supper. A huge dish of Wheaties, topped with slices of banana, heaps of dark brown sugar, and milk; my dessert was a Thomas' English Muffin with butter in every "nook and cranny." Of course Mom had to stock the shelves, but then she was out of the kitchen and I was eating whatever, whenever, and wherever I wanted. I either watched the Ed Sullivan show on our black-and-white TV or went to my room and ate by myself. A little snippet of solitude that Mom provided as I was growing up.

MARCH 19, 2011

I find myself spending a lot of time thinking about Mom. I'm too normal to be obsessing, but there's a quality of that. Suspended animation about something in my life—not the everyday tasks, but some way of being. I'm still my mother's daughter. When she dies something will shift, and I'll be alone and whole in a new way. I don't feel Mom is clinging on to me, but in some way I am clinging on to her. I want her to die because "it's time," but I also want her to live forever. The upshot is that I'm driving down to see her tomorrow. I know the visit will only be for a couple of hours but I have to do it, probably more for me than for her; but frankly, I think it's reciprocal.

MARCH 20, 2011

I'm back home exhausted, but glad I went. Two-and-a-half-hour drive each way. I was with Mom about three hours. We took a drive. When I pointed out the Wahackme Road house as we drove by, she looked, but then looked away, almost intentionally. I don't think she made any connection, nor did she recognize Alice and Dave's house as we drove by. I'd say that she enjoyed the ride as much as she can tap into any feeling, but really, we could have been anywhere. Back to Waveny for lunch, where she again organized all the little glasses and containers and ended up eating four carrots, four little pieces of chicken, one glass of cranberry juice, and a Dixie cup of ice cream. Big improvement, if that's the word, from my last visit.

Before heading home I stopped to see Alice and Dave. They seem to be doing fine. Dave's complexion was nice and rosy and he was enjoying the basketball March Madness.

MARCH 21, 2011

Thinking back, I must admit that yesterday Mom seemed sad, or shall I say lifeless. The spark had gone out of her.

How do I pray for a one-hundred-year-old woman whose external light is growing dim? This woman, my mother, was born with a joyful disposition and has always exhibited a deep inner peace, accompanied by a strong spiritual practice.

A year ago she told me that her favorite book was the Bible. These days she doesn't touch it. Her morning meditation ritual is gone. She can't put it together anymore; probably doesn't remember it; undoubtedly doesn't need it. In fact, I doubt that Mom needs any intercessory prayers from me, although pray I will. Her internal light is still glowing, and I know that God does not disappoint.

APRIL 4, 2011

My time at the cottage is coming to an end, at least for this season. So now what? Right now, as I sit on the deck looking out on a gray sea and sky, it is clear to me that "silence, solitude, and simplicity and sometimes being alone" are core issues for me, and for others, and that I want to keep blogging in some form even though I won't be at the cottage. But what might that be? On Thursday I will be locking the door for the last time this season. In many ways I am sad about it, but of course I know that nothing lasts forever. Dave is back in the hospital; Mom is fading away. Life at home gets busy with visitors, and in a few weeks I'll be going to visit sacred sites in Ireland with a group of women. My life journey will continue and new opportunities will come along. They always have and they always will.

APRIL 6, 2011

As I sit here on the deck watching my final evening come, I sense that indeed some of the silence, solitude, and simplicity I have been longing for have become part of me during these sixty-three days here. I should be able to create some variation of this wherever I go. No way do I want to take any of it for granted. But happily I return home, wondering if Mom will celebrate her one-hundred-and-first birthday.

APRIL 9, 2011
Dear Mom,

I'm thinking of you on this gorgeous spring day and can picture how beautiful it is out your window. On Sunday I am going to Ireland for a week with a group of women. I remember when you and I went there many years ago. We certainly had many wonderful trips together, didn't we? I return on April 19. Emily and family are coming for Easter, and I will come down and see you right after that.

I know you are praying for Dave. I feel so bad for him and for Alice. We must "pray without ceasing" for the entire situation. I thank God every day for you. You have always been the best mother for me, and I will never forget that. I am so grateful for you.

As Aunt Bow used to say, "I love you lots,"
Bobbi

APRIL 10, 2011
A new chapter, a new journal. The cottage is locked up, but I feel new possibilities opening up. Where to go and what to do with my travels? Definitely alone. Isle of Skye in late August? Iona, of course. Do I dare take three weeks? I'm always uplifted when I have plans. Some kind of wanderlust, travel-lust, in me. Of course there is Mom's situation to consider, as well as Dave's. Regardless, it's essential that I feel I have a purpose that I can share out there in the world.

APRIL 11, 2011
Here I am, a woman who loves solitude, about to spend a week in Ireland visiting sacred sites with thirty-five other women. What was I thinking? For one thing, I am continually reminded that I am an eager extrovert as well as an enthusiastic introvert. I figured that after my extensive introverted cottage time, it might be good to gain some balance through a

bit of concentrated time with others. Something about staying in balance. And anyway, I love to travel.

Sacred sites, be they in Ireland or at the cottage, are tools for soul work. They help with those soul questions, however I might frame them. Why am I here? What is my life purpose? What is my purpose at this moment in my life? Always important issues for me, but especially so as Mom fades and my purpose to make her happy goes with her.

APRIL 13, 2011
It's a challenge to experience silence on a trip with thirty-five women. Breakfast in silence helps, and we now have a couple of tables designated for those who want dinner in silence. I was one of three who sat there last night. What does that say about me? Silence on the bus covers the continuum. Some people are quite chatty and probably do not realize how easily their conversations travel up and down the aisle. I notice that those who sit in the back are quieter and more contemplative.

APRIL 18, 2011
The official tour is over but I'm still in Ireland. This pilgrimage has offered quite a contrast to all the silence, solitude, and simplicity I experienced at the cottage for nearly five months. Was the trip worth it? Of course. Besides visiting some awesome sites, I made several simpatico friends and solidified some ways of being for myself. But I doubt I'll ever join a tour again.

APRIL 25, 2011
Every day I pray for peace for Mom, but I don't think she really needs that prayer. She *is* peaceful—always has been. And yet, of course, she needs the prayers, or at least I need to pray them. Today she was full of smiles because Emily and Abigail visited her. She commented that it is good to smile and be grateful. No wonder I love to visit her. She lifts my spirits and makes me smile.

APRIL 26, 2011
The Mom Report
Dear Siblings,

I took Mom to the Inn and she sat outside while many of the staff came out and chatted with her. Well, they chatted and she did a lot of waving and smiling. Back at Waveny, as lunch was ending, Emily and Abigail came by on their way home. Mom really got animated and alive with them. She noticed something on Abigail's shirt—she still can read without glasses—and gave them many hugs. Definitely knew Emily. It was amazing how she keeps perking up when she sees people she knows and when there is activity personally directed toward her. Everyone does a good job of keeping her going at Waveny, but there's nothing like family.

Love,
Bobbi

APRIL 28, 2011
Margot visited Mom and reported that she was very vague and dismissive, and that taking her to church next Sunday, which will be her one-hundred-and-first birthday, or anytime for that matter, would be meaningless to Mom and would put her on display—the last thing we'd want to do. Of course this is what we had decided a few weeks ago, but I guess we have to revisit some of our decisions. Because church means so much to Mom, it's hard for me to accept that she will never attend another Sunday service. I doubt that it is in her consciousness and *that's* what's important.

MAY 2, 2011
Dear Mom,

It's a beautiful day in Sudbury. I love watching the budding leaves and flowering bushes bursting forth. You picked the most beautiful time of year to be born, Mom. And then you gave birth to four healthy children. How blessed you and Papa were and how blessed we all are.

Jim and I are coming down on Friday to wish you a happy birthday and to see Dave and Alice.

I'm still thinking about that wonderful visit you, Emily, Abigail, and I had a week ago. Four generations of women. I think of you every day and am so grateful that you have been my mother for so many years.

"Take delight in the Lord and he will give you the desires of your heart." Psalm 37.4

Love,

Bobbi

MAY 8, 2011

Great birthday celebration with Mom yesterday, the actual day being today, one hundred and one years ago. Alice was glad we brought a big cake so she didn't have to rally with all the particulars. She's done that so many times. Now it's someone else's turn. Mom was surprised and delighted as various family members arrived. I don't think she remembered it was her birthday, but she immediately got the message. Of course, Mom being Mom, she wanted us to share the cake with all her "friends and helpers," but mainly she just smiled her easy smile; smiling is what she does; the love behind her smile is who she is. She has had a good life, accompanied by some sadness, but all in all she exudes a life of one hundred and one grace-filled years filled with children, grandchildren, and friends.

How is it, *why* is it that this mother of mine has been blessed with a winning smile and all that goes with it? Theological questions abound. Are we born with certain dispositions, or do we cultivate them? What choices can we make about it? Where does grace come in? What about free will? I could go on and on, but this I know and have come to believe: Mom was blessed with a lovely disposition; God called her to bring love to others; and she chose to do it, she answered the call.

If anyone dares to wonder whether Mom has lived too long, or questions what her purpose is at this point in her life, just watch the love, joy, and hope that she smiles on everyone she meets. Talk about purpose in life!!

MAY 19, 2011

How can I make sense of what's going on in my family right now? On Mother's Day Mom celebrated her one-hundred-and-first birthday, while three miles down the road, in the very same town, my brother-in-law signed on to hospice at home. I was seventy-one in December, Emily will be forty-one tomorrow, and Abigail, ten in June.

MAY 26, 2011
The Mom Report
Dear Siblings,

Jim and I found Mom napping in the TV room, about to be awakened and taken to the ever popular Thursday cooking class. Today it was pizza. While she was helped to the bathroom, I cleared out some of her laundry and winter clothes, per order of Laundress Alice. Workmen were putting up a shelf in her room, so Mom and I walked to the recreation room and sat down for a little chat.

"I'm so glad to see you. I'm so glad you've come," she reiterated several times. When I told her we were planning to stop by the Jennings and then to go to Emily's, she looked right at me and said she was sorry Dave wasn't well. I think she thought he was still in the hospital. I straightened that out—maybe, maybe not. Regardless, she showed her compassionate, other-directed self.

I then proceeded to clear out her pocketbook, which held cookie crumbs, her wallet, four lipsticks, two compacts, and an array of paper napkins. Next, the bag on her walker, which was filled with letters, pictures, envelopes, cards, a dried-up bite of pizza wrapped in a napkin, emails, more napkins, and several knives, also wrapped in napkins. As she placed one under her sweater, she said, "I need them just in case." Whatever that means! I think letter opener, something she's used all her life. We all know that mail was always important to her.

When a woman came by wearing her bright green, flowered volunteer smock Mom said to me, "I should have worn my volunteer jacket." I asked her about volunteering and she said, "Yes, I volunteer every Friday. I do whatever is needed and then count the money."

As I finished the purse purging, one of the Get-About drivers came by to say hi and then Mom fell asleep, which was what she was doing when Jim came in. Although I think she would have been happy to stay right there and nap, we took her to the pizza making.

Oh, Mom has a new walker, one with wheels, so she doesn't have to lift it with each step. Her aide Michelle said that she is walking much more slowly these days. Other than that she is doing fine, happy, content, and quite wonderful. Everyone loves her there.

Love,
Bobbi

JUNE 10, 2011
Trying to sort out my sadness about my visit with Mom. I hardly had a moment with her because some friends came by to see her and we all—all with the exception of Mom—went to Alice's for lunch. It felt as if everyone was in a hurry to get away from the place, from this dear old woman, to blot out pictures of her aging and just remember the vibrant, smiling, welcoming lady she was. At the time I got swept up in the plans of the moment as though there were nothing

else I could do. In retrospect, I should have stayed with her. Anyway, I hate that we had to leave so quickly; hate that we can't communicate with her, hate that I can't make her happy, which is my job; hate that she is alone (although probably not lonely); hate that I can't see her daily and bring her some kind of joy that she can show and feel; hate that she is old and fading away from me; hate that she has to hang on. This feels more like sadness than guilt, but certainly some anger at the way things are. Maybe a part of me wanted to hurry away.

JUNE 17, 2011

With Mom fading away, family roles and structures are shifting. For some reason this gets me thinking about the value and necessity of sacrifice, as in "to make sacred." Visiting is sacred *and* sacrificial in that sometimes I'd rather stay home than visit someone who has no choice but to stay home. Although Mom admitted that there were times when she would have preferred not to pay a visit, she went anyway. I bet she didn't analyze it like I do. Visiting, reaching out, were part of her very fabric. She knew it was the right thing to do and off she'd go. It's in my fabric, and in Alice's and Margot's as well. I can be childish about it and stay home. Of course, I still *am* a child at age seventy-one. I still have a mother.

JUNE 21, 2011
The Mom Report
Dear Siblings,

Beautiful morning, nothing on my calendar, a good night's sleep, so off I went to New Canaan. Mom was in the TV room "watching" the French Open. She recognized me, asked about Jim, but for the first time ever didn't seem concerned about how he was managing without me. She looked so sweet in her baby-blue sweater and short haircut—no need for a perm. I wonder when that one lone front tooth will disappear *and* where it will go. *Don't ask*, I tell myself.

Mom was agreeable to taking a drive, so off we set. Again we exchanged some humor about the name of Frogtown Road and then there we were, approaching 371 Wahackme Road. A gardener was working over by the terrace so I decided to pull in and take a better look. Mom wasn't very interested. I wonder if she even knew where she was, that this was the family home?

Next stop, the New Canaan Inn. Mom wanted to get out, so we did, and sat on one of the benches out in front. She recognized several of the residents and helpers. Pilo was out working, and then Delilah, Ann, Barbara, and Candi appeared to say hello. David Brown [*our doctor growing up*] came over and wondered why those little growths on Mom's nose couldn't just be snipped off. "Once a doctor, always a doctor," I think. He and his wife live there now and he has tried to get a little vegetable garden going, but unfortunately, because of Board of Health regulations, the kitchen can't serve his produce. So I became the recipient of two heads of Boston lettuce.

Mom wondered if we were going to stay and eat. No, back to Waveny. On the way I stopped in the circle of the church driveway and pointed to the memorial garden that Dad designed and noted that his ashes are buried there. Not much of a response! When I asked her if she missed church, she said, "Oh, I go sometimes. Different people pick me up." For her purposes, she is still attending. Don't you love it? What an easy way to live!

Lunch at Waveny. I bought chicken, rice, and zucchini, and ate Mom's mushroom bisque and some, no, most of her carrot cake. Actually I could have had her entire lunch minus the two bits of chicken and the piece of the carrot cake that she carefully cut into six little sections, wanting me to take a piece to Jim. The word is that she isn't eating anything to speak of. I assured nurse Mary Ann and the nutritionist that we are fine with whatever Mom eats as long as she is comfortable. I'm aware that they have regulations to follow—offer three square meals each day—as well as families who might be upset that their loved one isn't eating.

The other medical issue I wonder about is Mom's walking. She is very slow and needs to be helped up from the chair. Clearly there would be a shift in her physical stamina, her heart, muscles, and so on, if she transferred to a wheelchair. Would that be okay? I think so.

Mom is definitely the grand dame of Waveny. When she points to where she wants to sit at a given meal, *that* is where she sits. When I tell people that as a mom she wasn't at all bossy, they are incredulous. But they also get that she is a kind person. She always says thank you and everyone knows that she means it. I must say that she is getting the best care ever, and she deserves it. Of course she has Laundress Alice, thank goodness.

Love,
Bobbi

JUNE 22, 2011

Thinking more about my visit yesterday. Mom's world is so small, but she still knows who I am and thanked me several times for coming. She can't hear unless I speak clearly and loudly and look right at her. Her one-hundred-and-one-year-old brain doesn't make many connections or remember much from the past, so very few words pass between us. But she reads my lips, smiles, says thank you, and holds my hand.

I am not advocating that people live as long as Mom, at least not as a goal. But, for those living into those later years, when they can't make many decisions or take care of all their personal needs, Mom offers a breathtaking example of how to sit in peace. More than that, she provides all of us with a simple way to be with very old people.

As I was leaving, just when I thought I had her all figured out, she asked, "Do you have your keys?" A truly prayerful, parental comment. Clearly it made the visit for me. Giving and receiving doesn't get any better than this.

JUNE 23, 2011
This week I've been visiting some church friends who can't get out easily on their own. Here I am, choosing solitude and cottage-by-the-sea time, and these folks are alone because their choices are limited. They can't get around like they used to. They've had to give up their driver's license and some are now relying on a walker or a wheelchair to maneuver about. And that doesn't even touch on memory loss. What gets to me is that in my own life I take for granted what these people *don't* have, namely a free rein of choices, at least as far as mobility is concerned. I want to believe that they feel some satisfaction from some of the other choices in their lives. Today during my visit to Norma, I got an answer: "I am thankful I have the choice to stay in my own home rather than go to a nursing home."

There's a good possibility that someday someone will be visiting me. I hope they will but not yet, because I still have to visit Mom.

JUNE 25, 2011
Tim, Emily, and grandkids come on Friday for a week of Camp Fisher. Jim has worked hard on the yard and getting all the activities in order. I'll gear up as camp cook. Won't have much solitude, but that's fine with me. I've very grateful.

JUNE 28, 2011
I've been going through the treasure trove of papers from Mom's active days with the church—around 1960. What a window into her faith—prayers she wrote, services she lead, activities with the Women's League and Lend-a-Hand, state-

wide activities, and more. This was before women "worked," when women in the suburbs still considered homemaking and volunteering a worthy job/profession.

This window into Mom's faith is personally sustaining, particularly at a time when although she is fading, she is still very much alive. While growing up and then when in college, I never doubted that Mom felt fulfilled in these volunteering/ church roles. Now, reading these prayers and the notes from the little talks she wrote for both local and statewide church-women doesn't have me changing my mind. Her Christian faith guided her life and she wanted to share the Good News with others. This was her true volunteer work.

Here is one of her prayers, written on the back of an envelope dated April 29, 1961. She knew that there was a connection between an open heart and the peace in the world:

> *We pray that we may have understanding in our relationships with those we work with, in our homes, our church, or community. We would ask for patience and an earnest desire to understand the needs and motives of our feelings, grow in our hearts and minds, so that mistrust or doubt and dislike may be rooted out.*
>
> *We pray for the success of the conference on Laos, that peaceful, fair solutions may progress in that divided country. Be with the delegates around the conference table.*

JUNE 30, 2011
The Mom Report
Dear Siblings,

I visited Mom today. When I walked into the TV room, she was asleep, waiting for someone to lead her to the next activity. She awoke with my touch and gave me her surprised look of recognition. Being with her is easy as long as I don't expect much in the way of conversation or response. I looked through the bag on her walker and threw away five or six used paper napkins that she had stashed away since my last purging, and showed her some of the birthday cards she had received two months ago. Her eyesight is excellent, so I pointed to the words and names and she nodded in some kind of recognition. She was more distant than even a week ago; content, not sad, just there. She had trouble remembering how to sit down.

We went to the Wednesday church service and took communion together. That would be a lovely last memory, a final gift, for I felt that perhaps it might be the last time I will see her.

Alice and I attended the regularly scheduled meeting about Mom. We have taken her off Synthroid, the only med she's ever taken, so now she is med free. Alice offered a final gift, to Mom, to herself, to me. She told the nurse in charge, "You know, our mother has never said a unkind word about anyone."

Love,
Bobbi

JULY 3, 2011

I'm trying to stay above the fray and enjoy all the usual family-life drama that happens here around every July 4th. Kids and grandkids went to the beach yesterday. Jim and I stayed home and at first I thought, "Oh, we should have gone." But I let go of that pretty quickly, realizing I'm rather comfortable being seventy-one—a retired, calm presence— ha! Tomorrow will be busy enough with the road race, lunch, parade, and cookout. I'm camp chef, which really means being in charge of the food but not doing much of the cooking.

JULY 6, 2011

Alice reported that Mom attended the weekly communion service at Waveny. It was the week for the Catholic priest to officiate, and although Mom is Protestant, that doesn't matter. She sleeps through each service, but that doesn't matter either. I hope the priest gave her communion, because *that* does matter to her. But on second thought it doesn't matter one iota. God is mysteriously wonderful, communion or no communion. God finds everyone in ways too wonderful for me even to imagine. Without a doubt, God has found Mom. In fact God found Mom one hundred and one years ago. And now they are two small voices whispering together again.

JULY 9, 2011
Another successful Camp Fisher. Now I'm back to my solitude. I feel some relief about life. How strange! Some desire, readiness, for Mom to go. She is ready, I am ready, we are all ready. Why do I feel it could be today? And yet I don't feel the need to go down to see her.

JULY 16, 2011
I made the round-trip visit to Mom yesterday. She recognized me but her life spark just wasn't there. According to the nurse, she is eating and drinking very little and they have put her in a wheelchair because she can't maneuver with her walker. As the Psalmist tells us, "Though I walk through valley of the shadow of death, I shall fear no evil." That's where I feel Mom is. I talked with Chris [*one of Mom's ministers*] about plans for her service and gave her a file folder filled with Mom's prayers and the worship services that she conducted back in the fifties for the Women's League. Her handwriting was as perfect as her typing. A treasure trove of insights into her life of faith.

JULY 21, 2011
Margot called last night after her visit to Mom—very thoughtful of her, because she knew how much I wanted her

Mom report. She said Mom was very dear, recognized her but couldn't come up with her name. They mainly sat and Mom looked at her and smiled. It took forever, but with her walker she made it to the dining area for tea. She didn't take one bite of her cookie and after a sip of tea said it was hot. That and "How's Dave?" were her only words.

I will go down on Monday and spend late morning and have lunch with her. That will be my only plan for the day.

"What will this day be like? I wonder." I remember that from *The Sound of Music*. Today I'll visit Barbara, who has been moved to her "last home" in the memory care unit of the facility where she has been living for the past few months.

JULY 25, 2011

Tim and I met just south of Hartford and rode together to visit Mom, arriving just as bibs were being passed out and lunch was being served. Mom seemed happier and more with it than during my visit ten days ago. She didn't speak much, but smiled a lot and seemed in tune with us. Tim activated that twinkle in her eye. She recognized him right away, although later may have had him confused with Jim. She ate one nibble of dessert and had a sip of apple juice and coffee. The aide told me that she had eaten a little breakfast, clearly her best meal. Before we left, Tim and I walked her to the TV room, which is the gathering place for her cohort. An aide would be coming to get her and take her for a nap. As Grammy said, "I am well," and I believe she is.

JULY 27, 2011

So looking forward to Scotland. Two full weeks on Skye at a self-catering cottage. More of a spiritual journey than a phys-ical adventure. I sense that my trip will be about saying good-bye to Mom and to some extent to parts of my busy, tenured, in-this-world life. I just have to believe that the trip is the right thing to do, whether Mom stays or travels home.

AUGUST 1, 2011

For the past four days I've been on a whirlwind of—well, I don't know what to call it, let me just say Intensity. Two funerals, one for a young man in his thirties, the other for a man in his late seventies. Then the round-trip visit to Mom, which included attending, with Alice and Margot, visiting hours for Clara, Alex's daughter. So sad. Alex did gardening at our house while I was growing up. He and Dad would work side by side. A beautiful friendship. When Dad died, Alex came by the very next day to see Mom and me. And now his middle-aged daughter has died of cancer.

Mom knew me, smiled, and told me, "I'm glad to see you." We sat for a while holding hands. She gazed out the window, and then promptly nodded off. Oh, to fall asleep as easily and peacefully! I pray for Mom many times a day, but she may be the last person on the planet needing prayers right now. She has always been one of God's blessed and that is still apparent at the twilight of her life.

While I was visiting, a friend of hers stopped by to say hi and leave the church bulletin. Mom waved but didn't pick up the bulletin, which she doesn't need or read anymore. The church service is in her heart, and she just smiles, waves, and winks the message out to those fortunate enough to be within her spiritual aura.

I am grateful, however, for all the church friends that stop by to see her. She may not remember that they came but their presence sends God's love whirling around the facility where she lives; the visitors then take that love out into their worlds, and on it goes. It even finds its way to me, and I do my best to share it with people in my arena.

Although yesterday's trip involved a good deal of activity and conversation—in the car, out of the car, greeting, hugging, crying, sharing memories—in the in-between spaces I was able to experience silence, solitude, and simplicity. As I held Mom's hand, and as I went through the bereavement line for Clara, I was aware that we were all standing alone together—in emotional yet peaceful solidarity.

AUGUST 12, 2011

Mammogram center called yesterday to ask that I return for a retake and an ultrasound on my right breast because they noticed some "thickness." I wasn't surprised, because it's happened before, but it jolted me. Brings up all kinds of thoughts centering around Mom.

She is getting ready to let go; am I mirroring her? My job to make her happy is about over, so what is my life purpose? I don't have to choose between living in the moment and letting go of life, but since my fiftieth high school reunion, in 2007, I've been living in that in-between space. In all honesty, my life purpose has been "waiting" for Mom to go. I keep visiting her, not knowing what else to do. But today I am *not* going down. I'm ready for her to go, and I have to fade away and let her do so in her own independent way. At a glance, this may appear brutal, but I have to let go some more, or shall I say I have to choose life.

I'm at a crossroads. Two roads diverging. I have the choice to follow Mom or choose life. I want both. But for sure my life path is through solitude. So here I am, imagining a clear breast, no thickness.

AUGUST 14, 2011

I went to see Mom yesterday. So much for holding off. She called me by name, and while gesturing toward me, said to one of her helpers, "My daughter." That was about it for words. However, I wrote out a couple of messages to her, which she read slowly, before nodding in acknowledgment. As I left I pointed back and forth between us, mouthing, "You, me," and then she winked. That's why she's here, to wink, to pass it on to the rest of us, certainly to me, but also to everyone else, however they receive it. She is teaching me to be grateful, to choose life, and *that* is what I must live for.

Yippee! The cottage is available, and Al and I are going for our third win-win season. For another season he and I will benefit from the silence, solitude, and simplicity of the cottage, as I keep it occupied, heated, and shoveled during the five winter months. We figure that this is probably the most simple rental arrangement on the planet—well, at least on the East Coast.

AUGUST 15, 2011

Today's great news at the mammogram center—I'm all clear: "We'll see you next year. No need to do the ultrasound." I'm very relieved. Right then and there I "teared up" and told Angela, the nurse, how grateful I was, because my one-hundred-and-one-year-old mother is about to leave this world and I'm so connected to Mom. Then I told her that Mom winked at me when I visited last time. I went on to say that I'd considered that maybe I wanted to leave with Mom, and breast cancer would be a way to do it. Angela said, "No, you don't want to do that, but I can understand how that thought could come up." What a good listener! Actually, that thought of leaving with Mom could be an unconscious one, but I'm working it through and getting back my purpose for living. Another thing: no more mammograms for me. Among the many reasons to call it quits is that I am too old.

Aches and pains never got in Mom's way, and for that she has always been grateful. Gratitude and humility go hand in hand; you can't have one without the other. Clearly Mom has both. I have miles and miles to go regarding each, my biggest learning lesson being humility.

Mom's legacy to me, to all of us: reach out, visit people, smile, be strong in your convictions, be grateful, be humble. She offered no judgments on lifestyle. I'm clear that I need a lot of solitude and time to be with myself. Although Mom had just that in the twenty-five years after Dad died, unlike me, she didn't choose it. We're different that way.

AUGUST 19, 2011
This week I have visited four church people, all who have dementia. Mom doesn't remember much, but I don't consider that she has dementia. She's just old and her brain is slowing down.

AUGUST 21, 2011
Next week, if plans go according to schedule, I will have landed in Glasgow, taken a bus to Ft. William, driven myself through Glen Shield, crossed over the Skye Bridge, and arrived at Siskin House, the cottage I've rented for two weeks. I wonder what I'll discover at this cottage near the sea? Before coming home on September 16, I also will have spent spend four nights on Iona.

My grandfather emigrated from Glasgow, and my mom used to tell us that this made her father a "Glaswegian." When I'm in Scotland, I imagine myself standing in the door of a croft looking out to sea. I feel that pull that says, "You're home."

I traveled to Scotland way back in 1955, with Mom, Dad, and Alice, then in 1986 and 1995, with Mom after Dad died, and once in 2006, with Jim and another couple. In 1996 I took my first solitary trip there, with Skye one of my destinations.

AUGUST 23, 2011
Emily, Colin, and Abigail stopped to see Mom on their way home after visiting us. I met them there, making the usual round-trip. We took a memorable picture of the four generations of women, plus another with Colin. Emily welled up seeing how much her grandmother had changed since Easter when she and Abigail had visited. Colin pushed Grammy's wheelchair around, and then we sat with her for a bit before they headed on to Lancaster.

I stayed for lunch. Mom doesn't feed herself anymore, but took two of the tiniest bites of cake and one sip of cranberry juice that I offered. Evidently she drinks a half a cup of Ensure twice a day. She asked, "How's Jim?" and that was about it for words. I decided *not* to tell her I was going to Scotland. If it registered with her at all, it would only confuse her.

When I get home from the trip, Mom will be in this world or she'll be in that other world. I'm at peace and have it all worked out with Alice and Margot that if Mom dies while I'm away, they will email me but I won't come home. We will schedule her memorial service when it is convenient for the family to gather.

I'm intense about the trip. I have a certain amount of guilt about wanting to live in solitude. It's not my family's kind of thing to do. But I'm so excited and it's what my heart desires. Acknowledging who I am, telling the truth to myself, following my bliss, are all challenges. So here I am, two days before I head off to satisfy my longing.

AUGUST 28, 2011
Easy flight to Philly. People on the Glasgow flight were relieved to fly away from Hurricane Irene.

Today on Skye I have walked in the wind, experienced intermittent sprinkles, and returned to my cozy cottage near the sea and to a warm bath; I have heard of power outages, flooded cellars, as well as loving acts of kindness happening back at home in the wake of Hurricane Irene. So strange to have flown away from it all.

AUGUST 30, 2011
Wish I had a view of the sea; this is a different experience, this cottage *near* the sea, not my cottage *by* the sea. Every day I want an excursion, but underneath it all is a way of being for me. This call for solitude is the next phase in my life, coming from the way I played alone as a kid, the way I socialized in

school, my mothering of Tim and Emily, my teaching career, divinity school and hospice work, and now back to childhood play. I see Mom's life with a similar pattern, and now she is showing me the final peaceful chapter. I seem to be preparing for it, but it is not a life crisis.

SEPTEMBER 9, 2011

Received an email from Margot. Mom stays in bed more of the time.

People are visiting and holding her hand. According to the nurse, she doesn't like to be alone. "My time with Mom was lovely. She recognized me and, shrouded in her blanket, looked lovely. She mouthed, 'I love you.' I decided to just tell her all the things I wanted her to know—how she'd been a good, loving mother, how we will all always think of her with love. She nodded off twice; the last time I left."

Alice wrote that when she stopped by, Mom said, "I'm all right. I'm busy." There is Mom, still sending that "always be busy" message. I don't feel guilty about the trip, but I sure wish I could be holding her hand. There are lessons for me here: humility and surrender. I think my sisters are consciously protecting me from too many details about Mom—so I can have a good trip—although Alice did mention that Mom may have to have her rings cut off because her fingers are swelling.

I have to trust that it is God's incredible mercy, this being here while Mom is dying. I haven't had many harsh lessons in life but this is one of them, this letting Mom go, even at one hundred and one.

SEPTEMBER 14, 2011

So much to be thankful for today. Being on Iona, weathering Hurricane Irene and making it here. I made the last boat from Oban to Mull and Mull to Iona before the ferries took a three-day hiatus.

SEPTEMBER 17, 2011

Jim and I visited Mom today. She recognized us both. In fact she saw Jim first and knew who he was before she saw me. I sat with her at lunch. Lunch? She didn't take one bite of solid food, but took a single sip of milk and two of apple juice, and then lifted her glass for a little toast. So like Mom, the essence of life, such humor.

Before we left Jim and I wheeled her around outside and then sat for a while on the bench near the entrance. I wrote some messages, which she read slowly and deliberately, taking a moment and then responding with a nod and occasional word. I told her I had been to Scotland, mentioned the trips we had taken together and that she and Papa had traveled pretty much all over the world. A faint nod and smile.

The last message I wrote: "God has been with you all of your life."

"That's true." Pause. "Very grateful."

That's Mom. She said it all, all that she was feeling at this time in her life, all that she has always believed and known in her life.

SEPTEMBER 24, 2011

I think about Mom all the time, aware that her time is almost up. She may die today. Chris Delmar [*her minister*] emailed that Mom received communion on Wednesday at the weekly service. I'll be there next week with her. This is "Mom waiting time."

SEPTEMBER 25, 2011

I've been thinking about my desire for silence and solitude, my longing for God, whatever that means. Undoubtedly, some of it has to do with my life stage; many of life's usual practical details aren't important or necessary to me anymore; I have addressed them. But aging isn't the entire reason for these longings. It must have something to do with who I am and who I am with Mom.

Today I'm going down to sit with Mom and spend the night with Alice. We'll see what the future holds, but this is for now, for today. Mom has always had this longing for God and has been blessed with its fulfillment. Her peaceful aura tells me this is true. No doubt about it. Throughout her entire life she has participated in this deep God work, and I trust that that will continue right up until her end. What a privilege to witness.

SEPTEMBER 26, 2011

I'm with Mom. Out of the goodness of her heart Mom's aide had put her on the bed for a morning nap. She got up for lunch—a couple of sips of juice. Nurse Patti said that she is slowly fading, but nothing dramatic. She's not bedridden and still uses the toilet. I have to keep remembering that this is a lady who has taken *no* meds, except for Synthroid, during her entire life—well, maybe a dozen aspirin, another dozen Tylenol. That's it. Literally.

SEPTEMBER 29, 2011

There is so much going on, and yet not much going on. Which is it? We are not getting Mom up. She seems at peace and isn't in pain. She is well cared for and loved. We're signing her on for hospice so she can get a hospital bed and more nursing services. This morning I took a walk; the rain had just stopped; it was warm and moist—and peaceful.

I've been staying with her during the day and going to Alice's for supper and an early night's sleep. There is plenty of silence and solitude, but things aren't simple, because Dave isn't well. I think it helps Alice to have someone else in the house, to talk with and be there if the call should come during the night.

SEPTEMBER 30, 2011

It was right to come home for a night to regroup and get some balance. Jim and I went to the movies and then out to supper. In the morning I'll head down to Connecticut to be with Mom until she gives that final exhale. She is peaceful, but I don't want her to be alone, nor do I want to be alone without her until I have no choice. Oh, there are helpers and friends coming in and out of her room, but I want some family with her. Who knows what's really important—that I be with her for her sake or mine. I'm going with both.

OCTOBER 1, 2011

I got here at 8:15 this morning. The nurse said that Mom had had a restful night. Right now she is awake, lying there, staring into space, then staring at me. I just waved to her and she waved back and then looked away. She is peaceful but not relaxed. Strange combination, but that's what I sense.

There's a beautiful silence in the room at the moment. Classical music is playing in the background. Of course Mom can't hear it, but I can and it fills the room with just the right amount of life energy. Without it there would be a lonely void. Now that I think about it, maybe Mom *can* hear it. Who knows what's going on in Mom's mind/body/spirit. Whatever it is, she is still busy, eyes open; but for sure, she is peaceful.

Mom needs someone with her, some family member on watch with her here. I recall her telling me that that when she was dying she wouldn't want just any person there every minute "but I'd like you." Not a need but a desire. Yesterday hospice brought a foam bed and an aide came to sit with her for a couple of hours, giving me a chance to go for a walk. At this point I like that she has different company although she really doesn't respond. Friends from church come by. She is well cared for, receiving the love she gave all her life.

Alice came in and was so dear to Mom. She comes twice a day. She said it was easier to cook dinner for me than to do what I do, sitting here all day. Skip [*Mom's minister*] came earlier when Alice was here and said a nice prayer with all of us. Mom recognized him.

I am in the in-between. Thinking of Mom and when her service will be. Then I think of the cottage by the sea. I'm looking for solitude, but I can feel it will be a different kind of solitude when Mom is not here. I'm tearing up. But she is still here. It may take a few days, but I couldn't possibly go home and leave her here all day. Not that everyone isn't wonderful, but nothing like family. I think she likes not being alone.

OCTOBER 2, 2011

This morning I arrived here at 9:15 after attending the eight o'clock service in the chapel at church. Skip offered a lovely prayer for Mom. Mom's eyes were open when I arrived and they still are. She did her usual staring at me and held my hand, but now she is looking the other way and I think she may be going off to sleep. She doesn't seem to be moving her hands as much as she did two days ago. I'm also noticing a little more breathing activity. Alice came in and Mom reached out her hand to her, clearly recognizing her.

As I sit here, it is a good time for me to remember. After all, the only person I can think of is Mom.

Mom used to volunteer here, right in these halls; delivering the mail to the rooms was one of her last jobs, just a year ago. Many of the people who work here have memories of her smile and determination to do her job with integrity.

She started out as the Friday cashier in the employee cafeteria at lunch time. Just this morning Elizabeth stopped me in the corridor, and with a big smile on her face recounted the time Mom told her that she owed twenty-five cents more for her lunch. "Your mother brought back memories of my own grandmother, who in a loving but determined way never let me get away with anything."

Four years ago they had to find another job for her. Although she was still accurate to the penny, she was taking too long making change and taking precious time from the employees' thirty-minute lunch hour. "Well," retorted Mom, "they just need to be given a longer lunch hour." Mom was always advocating.

So they gave Mom the job of delivering the mail to the residents' rooms. She'd put the letters in the pocket of her walker and make the rounds. Nine months ago when she came here to live, she brought along her volunteer smock and had every intention of continuing her Friday volunteer job. But she soon forgot, along with many other routines that had been such an important part of her life. Now volunteers and those who work here are helping her.

Mom has had a plethora of prayers said with and for her over the past few days. Skip and Chris, her family, other visitors, and of course all of her friends, as well as mine from around the world, are all praying for a sweet passing. As I sit here, I truly believe that she is in the valley of the shadow of death where she feels no evil. I am "very grateful" for this time with her and for all the prayers. She is not alone; I am not alone.

OCTOBER 3, 2011
9:30: I arrived here about 8:30. Mom was lying there eyes open, and that's the way she is now. Her eyes look red and I think they put some moisturizer on them. I can hear her breathing a little, and once in a while she gives a little cough. Mainly she's just staring on ahead, although she is moving her hands more than yesterday. She seems quite alert but then morning has always been her best time. She looks at me but doesn't give me specific recognition. She seems to be looking at some beyond.

Margot called that she is taking the train, arriving here by 5:00, depending on which train she catches. I let out a sigh of relief, for Mom, for Margot, and for all us. I'm sure she'll be glad that she made the effort. Sarah [*Margot's daughter*] is coming too. Ross is so far away, but he and Mom are connected in spirit.

12:30 p.m.: The hospice nurse came by and told us that Mom is into the active dying process. Maybe tonight. She's going to give her some comfort meds after Margot arrives, which, at last report, will be by 3:00. At the moment she is breathing rapidly, looking all around, very intense. They will set up a bed next to her so I can spend the night. The plan is to go to Alice's for supper and then return here.

4:00 p.m.: Sarah drove in from Boston a while ago to join Alice and me, and then Margot arrived from D.C. She spoke with Mom, who was alert and active, definitely recognizing her. When we were "ready," the nurse gave some morphine. Mom settled down.

6:00 p.m.: We left Mom sleeping deeply and went to Alice's for supper.

7:20 p.m.: As we were preparing to return, the call came to the house that our mother had died. In tears I made a call to Ross, Tim, and Emily. Alice, Dave, Margot, Sarah, and I returned and gathered around Mom's bed. She was still warm. We said a prayer; we cried; we told stories; we said we didn't have a mother anymore; we said we were "very grateful" and we were. When we were ready, the funeral home was called. I waited until she left the room. That's all I can write.

OCTOBER 4, 2011

Here's what I wrote to family and friends:

> Our dear mother died on October 3, 2011, at 7:20 p.m. She lived one hundred and one years, four

months, and twenty-five days. My sisters and I were with her just an hour before she passed, and my brother, who lives in Portland, Oregon, was with us in spirit. Everyone knew that my mom was a saint, everyone that is except Mom. She was the most beautiful person in the world and the most important person in my life. I feel blessed to have had her for close to seventy-two years.

We will be remembering Mom and celebrating her life at the Congregational Church, New Canaan, Connecticut, on October 22 at 11:00 a.m.

OCTOBER 5, 2011

I spent eight days at Mom's bedside, holding her hand and advocating for her care. It was a blessing. Now I'm home. I went to bed at 9:00 and was up a little after 5:00. I'm refreshed and giving myself four days of silence, solitude, and simplicity. *No* plans with anyone, *no* obligations.

I remember those last words Mom and I shared just thirteen days before she died:

"God has always been with you all of your life."

"It's true—very grateful."

How's that for a blessing?

OCTOBER 6, 2011

I journey on. All good, but hard to settle down. Right now I am in another one of those in-between places, between Mom's death and her service. Lots to do, with much back and forth among the sibs about her service. It's been healing to work with her church, discussing which scripture to include. Mom had suggested Isaiah 6. 1–8, Matthew 24.31–45, and Psalm 91. Psalm 121 (King James version) will be read at the committal service in the church memorial garden following the service.

Reading some of Mom's papers. On the back of a sheet of paper on which she had written "2003," she recorded the significant years of her life, first her birth, Vassar College, and marriage, noting her age at the time, and then the birth of her children (Alice, Bobbi, Margot, Ross) and their ages in 2003:

b 1910
VC 1931 – 21
m 1935 – 25
A 1937 – 66
B 1939 – 63
M 1945 – 58
R 1947 – 56

At the end of the list Mom wrote: "And when our work is done, our course on earth is run, may it be said, 'Well done; be thou at peace.'"—West Point Alma Mater

OCTOBER 7, 2011

Working on Mom's service—energized by it all. Last night it came over me that I am free, not of Mom, but free in a new way. Mom always gave me freedom. She never became overinvolved in my life. No helicopter mom, for sure. So what is this freedom? Well, physical freedom because I won't be visiting her. Free of some of the family *shoulds*, free to follow my own in a new way. My thoughts turn to the cottage by the sea, my trips next spring and fall, and this longing for solitude.

Now that I don't have the job of making Mom happy anymore, I'm free, because I don't have to do so for anyone else. I made her happy, did my part, right up to her end. Oh, I'll still be nice, but I'm released from that charge. Although Mom never clung to me, something I gave to her is now back in my possession. She gave it back before she died; she didn't need it anymore.

OCTOBER 8, 2011

Mom's final gift to me—well, besides the "very grateful" gift—was that she shared with me her struggle not to judge people. "We shouldn't judge; we just don't know what someone else is going through," she commented during one of our many conversations about life and about God. She tried hard not to judge or talk negatively about anyone. Her highly developed ethical sense of right and wrong and her Christian faith told her it was wrong. I don't believe she felt guilty about it. Rather, she prayed, asked for forgiveness, and went about humbly bringing light to everyone she met.

OCTOBER 10, 2011

Everyone, and I mean everyone, has only positive things to say about Mom. That's the way it's always been. You might think that would be hard to live up to, but I'm not trying to live up to my mother; I never have; she would never have wanted that. That was another gift to me, and I think to my siblings as well.

Mom was humble. She knew she wasn't always open-minded, but with God's help, she believed she could come close at times, at least close enough. And she believed in that possibility for everyone. God's grace was available for all. The message of that possibility was her gift to everyone who knew her, whether they were aware of it or not.

OCTOBER 17, 2011

When Mom's service is over, who will I be? I feel myself drifting away from some of the everydayness of life. I'm not depressed or feeling purposeless, but where will I, an orphan about to turn seventy-two, find meaning now that the most important person in my life is gone? No fear, just courage to pull away, to do it. I'll be going to the cottage in a month. I can't wait.

OCTOBER 18, 2011

A day to myself—My Day. I'm yearning for silence and a life of solitude and simplicity. Not to get away from anything but to live in that space. I want to do this alone, for myself, with no desire for anyone else in my life to embrace it. It's very personal, interior, and mysterious. I can work around it so that others, particularly Jim, can do what they need to do, which of course is my desire for all human beings. *Follow your bliss*. I have roles to play in the lives of family and friends, just as they do in mine. Hmm, I wonder how it will be with my siblings now that Mom is gone? Will we see one another more as sisters than as daughters sharing a mom? Ross, living far away and eight years younger than I am, will always be Ross.

OCTOBER 19, 2011

Rainy, dreary day here, this waiting time before Mom's service, on Saturday. When someone lives to be one hundred and one, there's no big need to have the memorial service immediately, as with tragic, sudden, untimely deaths. Mom's slow fading away, plus her age, helped us prepare for her parting, and so waiting for two and half weeks seems just fine and logistically sensible.

And yet the waiting. All the arrangements have been made—the service itself, hotel reservations, family gatherings, even what to wear. It's a restless time.

OCTOBER 22, 2011

All the family, except for Alice's gang, is staying at the Hilton Garden, in Norwalk. Last evening we took over a good part of the Italian restaurant next door, every immediate family member except for Ross's Kristin, who is in the Peace Corp, in Morocco. Our cousins John and Betty Jo drove all the way from North Carolina. So many stories. Everyone is doing what they need to do, being who they are. I'm trying to be a prayerful presence. I want to be with Mom today. Today is Jim's birthday; nineteen years ago the memorial service for his mother was on my birthday. Both days of gratitude; both women of generosity.

OCTOBER 24, 2011

Mom's service, as well as the family gathering, was more than I could have hoped for or imagined. And now I am home so desperately wanting solitude but not able to take it when offered. Today I'm meeting Sarah and Barbara [*daughter and sister of my college friend Sally, who died five years ago, at age sixty-seven*]. To think, Mom lived thirty-four years more than Sally did. What a mystery. Clearly, this is just the right thing for me to be doing today. And then the rest of the week is mine for silence, solitude, and simplicity, if I'm able to take it. I guess it will take a while for this adrenaline surge to subside.

Again and again I am taking in that Mom is not alive anymore. Do I dare open the floodgates?

OCTOBER 25, 2011

No question, all present at Saturday's service left knowing deep in their heart that gratitude guided Mom's life. Gratitude was the catalyst for how she led her life. Through the lens of gratitude Mom honestly and thoroughly examined and responded to every situation in her life, the commonplace and the eventful, the joyful and the sorrowful; and then she would move on, expressing gratitude for how God had worked for the good. The important point is that Mom's gratitude was not for any particular outcome but for the very fact that God had always been with her, in both the good times and the tough ones, at the start of her life and at its end.

Bobbi Fisher, 2011

Moving On

Let me abide in your tent forever, find refuge
under the shelter of your wings.
—Psalm 61:4

Mom has been gone three and a half years. Since her death, I have been trying to write the story of my amazing mother and what she gave to me, particularly in the last years of her life.

Now, after numerous drafts, countless walks, and much prayer, I have come to understand that, as Mom admitted with her final words, God was with her all her life. She was blessed with abiding faith during all her one hundred and one years. For that, she was very grateful—and *that* is the story I needed to tell.

Having done so, it is with gratitude that I move on with my life. I am seventy-five years old now, the same age as Mom when Dad died and she had to move on without him. My cottage-by-the-sea days, which I enjoyed for five winters, are over. What I learned during that time about silence, solitude, and simplicity I now carry with me wherever I go. My home is where I want to be, although I continue to travel and hope to do so for as long as I am physically and mentally able. Church offers worship and opportunities for outreach, friends keep me honest, my family helps me love and feel loved.

I continue to remember things Mom said and the ways she responded to people and situations. For me, her greatest gift was how she embraced old age and died peacefully with the same gratitude that had always been the foundation of her faith. For the first ninety-nine years she expressed this gratitude through words and actions. At the end, her smile said it all.

Like Mom, every morning I thank God for my family, my health, and my life. I listen with my heart to the memories as I move into my old age, I hope as gracefully as Mom did, so that at the end of my life I, too, will be able to say, "Very grateful."

www.ingramcontent.com/pod-product-compliance
Lightning Source LLC
Chambersburg PA
CBHW031320040426
42443CB00005B/165